MANAGING THE MIST

How to develop winning
mind-sets and create high
performing teams

ANDREW SILLITOE

Managing the Mist

First published in 2013 by
Panoma Press
48 St Vincent Drive, St Albans, Herts, AL1 5SJ, UK
info@panomapress.com
www.panomapress.com

Book layout by Neil Coe.

Printed on acid-free paper from managed forests. This book is printed on demand to fulfill orders, so no copies will be remaindered or pulped.

ISBN 978-1-908746-98-6

This book is available online and in all good bookstores.

In the memory of Hugh (Jock) Munn for the nights in the garage and teaching us what a winning mind-set really is.

Acknowledgements

Winning is great, but if you ask any athlete what the best part of playing team sports is they are likely to say 'the road trips'. I have had plenty, my most memorable with the Tunbridge Wells Street Cruisers; therefore I would like to acknowledge the team and that part of my life for the wonderful memories and amazing friendships I still have today. Two major European trophies and twice National Champions was simply a bonus.

Thank you to Mindy for her ability to help me remain focused and positive about writing a book. There were several times when my 'inner critic' was questioning why the hell I was writing a book; she kept me going, coaching me throughout the process.

Now to the people whose ideas, philosophies and courage have inspired me: Dale Carnegie for kick-starting my passion for personal development, Patsy Roddenburg for her wonderful book *Presence*, which has affected the lives of so many people. Daniel Pink for writing *Drive* and providing such incredible insights for us all to benefit from, and Malcolm Gladwell for his relentless and ground-breaking analysis.

Dr Colin Wallace for your contribution to the book, and thanks to Barry, Lisa, Charlie, Graeme, Andy and Alex at *PRISM* Brain Mapping for embracing me into your world.

A special thank you to Nathan Sage for recruiting me into my first consulting role. I had zero consulting experience and Nathan took a risk for which I am truly grateful.

Colin Gee for your attention to detail, support, challenging my ideas and helping to make this a better book.

Jock Munn for helping me believe in myself, inspiring me to do more than I thought possible and providing me with a competitive edge. His strength and determination will live in my heart forever.

Thank you Mum! I know you'll be reading this, so thank you for driving me to hockey and your unshakeable belief in me; you're an absolute Inspiration to me and so many people.

The two special people in my life who have been with me throughout writing this book, they never questioned my sanity or the times when I was locked away in my office for several months working on the book. My amazing daughter Izzie who lights up my life every day and Lucie who has been nothing but supportive, challenged my thinking and helps me to become a better person, I love you both.

PART THREE - STAY IN THE ZONE

PART FOUR - HAVE A STRATEGY

Introduction

In 2007 a consultancy that specialises in improving business performance asked me to deliver a keynote speech on the 'Winning Mind-set' at one of their teambuilding days. The Chief Operating Officer (COO) of the consultancy at the time was an old school friend of mine. We had not spoken in twenty years although he had been following my sports career. I grew up playing a relatively unknown sport, especially by English standards where most young children aspire to play football for England. I've had an unusual, albeit successful sports career competing and coaching all over Europe and throughout the United States and Canada. My sports career started on the car parks and playgrounds of Tunbridge Wells playing street hockey through to representing California at the highest level in Las Vegas at inline hockey. This book is a personal account of my experiences as a player and Head Coach for Team GB, and a set of practical tools for enhancing personal, team and business performance.

Despite my experience, when I sat down to write the speech it occurred to me that I wasn't entirely sure what a winning mind-set was. I knew what I had done to achieve my goals, the sacrifices I had made and the effort that had been required from me, but I wasn't clear on how to express that in a motivational or inspirational way. I sat down in a café with some strong coffee and started to write the speech. I had never been a person who excelled at writing essays or perceived myself as academic in any way; however, on this occasion I was like Forest Gump but instead of running, I was writing, and I kept writing and writing. Despite my best intentions to write a speech, I actually and unintentionally wrote my personal story. I surprised myself with my writing prowess which also resulted in quite an emotional experience. It has certainly been an eye-opener for me and I have chosen to be open and share my personal experiences with you in this book. If you ever get round to writing your personal story you will experience an interesting stroll down memory lane. It can be a painful and emotional experience, but very enlightening. I encourage leaders to write a short autobiography highlighting their highs and lows as part of my leadership programme. It is a powerful way to help define who you are, what you value and what is important you.

The reconnection with the COO, combined with the frustration that I couldn't clearly define what a winning mind-set was, caused me to spend the next six years researching and observing top performing athletes, leaders and teams. It was also the reason for changing my career and moving away from a successful sales career in media to a consulting role in 2007.

Whether you're a team manager, a business leader, a coach or an athlete you will find that the concepts and models in this book will equip you to enhance your personal performance, create high-performance teams and develop winning mind-sets. If you embrace them and make them your own you will go on to achieve more than you ever thought possible.

'Managing the mist' is an analogy for managing emotions and the ability to maintain clarity of judgement, particularly under stressful conditions. We have all experienced the 'red mist' or the 'white mist' at some time in our lives, either at work, playing sports or with friends and family. The mist is a reaction to anxiety, fear and stress. Our brains are designed to protect us in dangerous situations; however, as I describe in this book, this is not always necessary or conducive for achieving high performance. During these times of crisis we are often presented with an opportunity, but our lack of clarity distorts our judgement. Therefore your role as a leader is to manage the mist, achieving clarity, vision and alignment for both yourself and those you are leading.

The practical models have been developed to help you overcome the mist. They are based on my own personal experiences and what I have learned from other experts. They are tried and tested and are underpinned by neuroscience combined with extensive research into psychology. I have applied the models during the last five years, helping over 2,000 individuals design personal strategies to improve their own performance and the performance of others.

To help you navigate through the book it has been split into four parts. Part One explores what a winning mind-set is and identifies the three key principles for developing a winning mind-set. The following three parts are structured around the three principles. Part Two has a focus on self-awareness, Part Three pays attention to self-regulation and staying in the zone and part four provides insights into strategy and the rules required for creating a high-performance team and a mist-free environment.

I hope you enjoy reading it and find it useful; please feel free to email me, it would be great to hear from you.

andrew@managingthemist.com
www.managingthemist.com

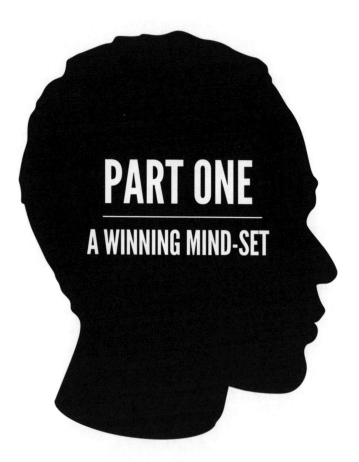

PART ONE

A WINNING MIND-SET

CHAPTER 1

HAVE A WINNING MIND-SET

What is a winning mind-set?

I have been obsessed with what drives and motivates human behaviour ever since I can remember. During the last ten years I have wanted to know the recipe for creating a team of winning mind-sets or even an organisation of winning mind-sets. Over the last 100 years we have seen the likes of Roger Bannister break the four-minute mile, Tiger Woods dominate at golf, Michael Jordan set a new benchmark in basketball. Teams like Manchester United consistently stay at the top of world-class football. Michael Phelps, Sir Steve Redgrave, Jessica Ennis, Bradley Wiggins and many more have amazed the world with their passion and drive to succeed.

I also wanted to know what drove the likes of Gandhi, Mother Teresa, Nelson Mandela, Martin Luther King and the unsung heroes who have done such great humanitarian work for completely selfless reasons. What was the connection between these people who have achieved so much in their own and others' lives? What was driving them?

I wanted to know what great leaders were doing to increase self-belief and followership in others. What is 'followership' and what does it really look and feel like? Have you ever followed anyone? Did they really lead you? What were they doing to create winning mind-sets and high-performance teams? I started to consider who had inspired me to achieve more and go beyond my own expectations. What did they say to me? How did they say it? It started to occur to me whether the idea of 'followership' really existed. My experience of great leaders was based on a participative approach, involving me, allowing me the freedom to make mistakes and learn. They rarely intervened in my activities, only making themselves available to hold me accountable for what I had committed to do. On reflection, they appear to me now as great facilitators of high performance. They trust and believe that everybody is resourceful, creative and capable.

During my career I have experienced a number of managers and coaches in both business and sports. Some were great, some were OK and others clueless. What was it that was separating these leaders? My management career started in retail. I left school at 16 with a handful of GCSEs. What I lacked in academic ability I made up for in ambition and drive (I didn't have a choice). I had a number of jobs from selling suits on the East London markets, managing a sports shop, owning a sports development company, to selling skis. I even spent some time laying tarmac on the streets of my local town before joining a FTSE 100 media sales company.

My management career didn't start well. I cringe at some of the behaviours I displayed. I challenge anyone who says management is easy. It is fair to say that I have had moments of greatness, been OK and been clueless. Management is hard and the sooner you accept this, the better manager you will become. The mistake I made was pretending it was easy and that I had it nailed. Being accountable for delivering results through people is a huge responsibility. At the same time, whether you are coach, leader, teacher, captain, parent or mentor, creating winning mind-sets is one of the most rewarding and satisfying things you can undertake; it is a way of life and constant work in progress.

I have learned that a winning mind-set is essentially an attitude of mind. With the right mind-set you will live, work and compete at your full potential. Virtually everything you do in your life is ruled by choices that you make. You can choose to focus on the negative or the positive; you can get stressed about things beyond your control or you can focus on the things that you can influence. An obstacle can be a barrier to performance or it can be an opportunity to learn and improve. These choices will have a direct impact on your performance and well-being.

After ten years of research and observations of top performers, I have come to the conclusion that there are three key criteria for creating a winning mind-set. Firstly, those who possess a winning mind-set have a high level of self-awareness, they know their strengths and weaknesses, motivations and their approach to taking risks. Secondly, they have the ability to manage their thoughts, feeling, emotions and behaviours, especially when under pressure, i.e. they can manage the mist. Thirdly, they are goal orientated and have a plan for achieving their goals, both personally and at an organisational level. The *Three Principles* have become the cornerstone of Winning Mindset Consulting's philosophy. I also believe they link success in both the business and the sports arena, and in fact all walks of life. *The Three Principles* should be applied together to achieve maximum output. *The Three Principles* are underpinned by neuroscience with the aim to provide academic rigour to the concept.

The Three Principles of a Winning Mind-set

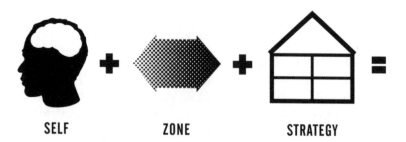

SELF   **ZONE**   **STRATEGY**

Be Self-Aware

The first principle is Self-awareness. Top performing individuals have a high level of self-awareness. Knowing your strengths, weaknesses, motivations and your approach to taking risks is key to your success. However, the biggest barrier to self-awareness is often ego. Unfortunately, many leaders are driven by their ego. Their desire to be right, never to be seen as vulnerable or making mistakes is the biggest inhibiter to bringing out the best in themselves and others. My ego has definitely got the better of me in the past and I have also been a victim of someone else's ego more than once. You must be careful not to get tripped up by your own ego; if you are driven by ego, you will find in time that letting go of it will be one of the most empowering and enlightening things you will ever do. This can happen late in someone's career but it is a choice that you can make. Leadership is a selfless act. If you want to achieve results through people to enhance your own status then leadership may not be for you. The results are merely a by-product of doing things right.

Being aware of your strengths and knowing how to exploit them will give you a competitive advantage. Too often we focus on weaknesses only to become less than average at our weaknesses and then neglect our strengths, reducing the impact of what we are great at. However, you should also be aware that an overused strength can become a weakness if not managed properly. Strengths can derail you and cause you to behave in ways that are not conducive for high performance.

Utilising strengths will make your team stronger. Strong teams are dynamic and have varying degrees of strengths. I have had the angelic view in the past that if I can improve the weaknesses in my team I will have a rounded, performing team. This is not always the case; in fact I would go as far as to say that it is never the case. We will talk about strengths in Part

Two and how top performing individuals and teams focus on strengths and why they are great.

Another important element of self-awareness is to know what motivates and drives you to succeed. Motivation is a hot topic when it comes to team performance and leadership. I have been referred to as a motivational speaker; it is not something that I am comfortable with. If my audience leaves feeling motivated then great, but it's not my intention to motivate. Motivation is far more intrinsic than hearing a few words from a keynote speaker. I have one goal as a speaker and that is to inspire the audience towards action. If there is one thing we can do in life it is to take action. Nothing happens without action; however, action is also associated with risk, and it is likely that you have a deep-rooted approach to how you manage risk. Your approach to risk will dramatically impact your opportunity for success and learning, whether you are impulsive or averse to risk. According to Geoff Trickey (2012), renowned psychologist and business consultant, being comfortable with risk is one of the most defining characteristics and is significant because any job involves risk of some sort.

Taking action or a risk can also be interrupted by a lack of motivation. Identifying with what motivates you is essential for achieving a winning mind-set. When I am asked how I motivate my team I reply by saying "I don't." I have a keen interest and curiosity for understanding what motivates them and I find this out by simply asking them. However, it is their responsibility to influence what motivates them in their life, as it is yours and mine. We will discuss motivation in more detail in Part Two.

Being self-critical and having high expectations is an important component when it comes to developing a winning mind-set although, as a coach, I find this can also be one of the most detrimental behaviours in an individual. Whilst being critical of your performance is important, it is also important to know that today you are 'good enough' and tomorrow you can be even better. Many people don't feel good enough today and lack confidence due to their perception of themselves. You probably have a voice in your head that doubts you. This is known as your 'inner critic'.

It's important to get to know your inner critic and become more familiar with the voice inside your head. Most people try to ignore it only to find that it appears when they least expect it. It can cloud your judgement and create the mist. Just when you realised your goal and a strategy, you hear a voice say "Yeah but" or "What if." It can create limiting beliefs and try to throw you off track. All top performers and entrepreneurs hear it, but what separates them is their ability to deal with it.

Ultimately, it is a distorted version of you that you have created through the environment you have grown up in; it is your conscious self. The inner voice is often referred to as the 'gremlins' or a 'bully'. I recommend that you give yours a name. Imagine what it looks like or draw an image of it on paper, try and make sense of it. You can also draw a positive image, identify with a friendly version, a positive advisor, maybe even how you see yourself in the future. This level of awareness is essential when working towards your goals. The voice will always be there so it may as well assist you in reaching your goals, rather than preventing you.

Stay in the Zone

The second principle and the area of performance that I am most often approached about is Stay in the Zone. Individuals and teams that perform at the highest level have the ability to manage their thoughts, feelings, emotions and behaviours; essentially, they are able to 'manage the mist' when they are under pressure. Being in the zone will enhance your gravitas, how you resonate with people, it will increase your awareness, clarity of judgement, decision-making and the ability to manage risk effectively. It will also define you as a person and your level of mental toughness. When I first started my career in performance improvement, the focus of my research was on how to 'get in' the zone. I now believe that we are all in the zone and the challenge is not getting into it, it is in fact staying there. There are moments in our life when we act irrationally and we later reflect on this experience wondering why it happened – sound familiar? It is simply a natural response to a perceived threat. The opportunity here is to rationalise the perceived threat and put it into perspective. The brain doesn't differentiate from one threat to another and therefore reacts accordingly. Top athletes are able to manage this, remain composed and maintain clarity in crisis; when there is crisis there is also opportunity. I talk more on this in Part Three.

Those with a winning mind-set have an undeniable self-belief which manifests itself as confidence, or at least it is perceived that way. You may be surprised how many top athletes and leaders are terrified on the inside but have developed the ability to give off an entirely different perception. They have learned how to manage their emotions and behave in a way that is required to perform at their best. The more they do it, the more habitual and easier it becomes. When I first started personal coaching I was incorporating hypnotherapy techniques to help clients get into a relaxed state. I rarely use hypnotherapy today, however there was one thing that really stood out for me when I was training to become a hypnotherapist, and this can be applied to any role.

To be credible I had to be convincing. When someone asked me if they could be hypnotised I'd respond with a positive "Yes of course" rather than a timid "I'll give it a go" even if on the inside I was feeling nervous about it. Whether it was during management training or at a party I would always offer a resounding "Yes!" I have even hypnotised an interviewer in an interview at a consultancy to prove the power of positive thinking (I got the job, by the way). I have even taken the liberty of sticking a colleague's foot to the floor at a team-building event. Without having an absolute belief or at least giving the impression that I am convinced I can do it, the results would have been different. This is the same in all walks of life. To be truly great at something you have to behave like you are great. Muhammad Ali was a master at this. He said: "To be a great champion you must believe you are the best. If you're not, pretend you are." Whilst he was an extremely talented boxer, he was also very confident and convincing about his ability – however, there is a fine balance between confidence and arrogance.

When I worked with traders in the city, one of the key factors for their development was to help them look, act and feel like a trader. It was quite a transition for them, as they couldn't see themselves as traders until they were successful and making money. The problem was they would never achieve their goals until they started behaving like a successful trader. It is the same for an amateur athlete wanting to become professional; to become professional they have to behave like a professional in the first place. You can adopt successful behaviour, you can assimilate positive behaviours in others and emulate them. If you are aspiring to achieve something, you'll need to act like it today. I have found this concept very powerful and it has been influential in achieving my personal goals.

Hypnotherapy is useful for getting into a relaxed state, and when you are relaxed you will have clarity and enhance your ability to make sense of your emotions. Although my clients were learning to manage their emotions more effectively, it didn't appear to be sustainable. It was a good business model because clients were returning, but ethically it felt wrong. I wanted my clients to experience sustainable change. I felt that my coaching required more substance, hence introducing strategy and self-awareness. Another key factor when developing the ability to stay in the zone is how you perceive a threat. The bigger the threat, the more cortisol is released in the body. Cortisol is the hormone related to stress that helps protect you in danger but is not necessarily useful for high performance. We will go into more detail in Part Three.

Have a Strategy

The third principle is strategy. Top performing teams and individuals know what they are aiming for, they have a purpose and they know how to get there. They have what I refer to as their 'House in Order'. Getting Your House in Order is a metaphor for creating a holistic strategy using a whole-brain approach. It requires having a vision for the future, a plan and an appropriate set of behaviours for achieving your goals. Whether you're leading a team or an individual wanting to improve your own performance, having a flexible and holistic strategy is absolutely crucial. Without a strategy you will fall short of achieving what you set out to do. You will be familiar with the adage "Fail to plan, plan to fail". Avoid failure by applying the approach I share with you in Part Four and you will go on to achieve more than you ever thought possible.

As an Olympic event comes to a close, an athlete will start to plan for their next event. This is one of the key differentiating factors between the mind-set of an athlete and a non-athlete: an athlete is constantly looking towards their next goal. They will have a vision which will be broken into smaller goals, a plan of execution and the right set of behaviours in place to drive performance. This is a characteristic that you will need to adopt to achieve high performance. A winning mind-set requires a relentless desire to succeed. I'm not suggesting that you never rest. Rest and downtime are essential factors for continuous improvement and should be included in your planning. I am often asked to help individuals with their time management. When I suggest to them that they should take at least another hour out of their time to do nothing except reflect, they think I am mad, but are pleasantly surprised at how much more efficient they become by building downtime into their diary.

Having a strategy is even more important when an athlete retires. Retirement from sport can be an extremely difficult transition, and in some cases causes severe depression. It is probably the biggest test of an athlete's mental strength. They are used to goal-setting and having a purpose. This must continue through life beyond their sports career. I have experienced this first-hand; it can be a dark and lonely place. My expectation is that there will be an epidemic of struggling retired athletes in the future if better support and career development isn't put in place. A strategy will give you a sense of purpose and direction. Without purpose the world can become a very unhappy place. As with motivation it is our personal responsibility to create purpose for ourselves. You'll need a vision for a desired future state, you'll need to know your strengths and what motivates you to take action. It's not always easy, but you are biologically equipped for survival, so take advantage of your innate winning mind-set and go for it. We get one shot at this life and today is the start of the rest of it.

Firstly, you will need to be goal orientated and have a plan for achieving your goal. This may come naturally to you or you may be someone who isn't necessarily results driven. If you are in the latter category you will require more focus and perhaps it will take you out of your comfort zone. Either way, it is absolutely essential that you have a result in mind and a strategy for getting there. We will discuss how to create a personal and team strategy later in the book.

Having the right mind-set and belief for achieving goals is the difference between winning and losing. Having a winning mind-set is not about being ruthless, stubborn or suppressing emotions. It requires openness to change, embracing failure rather than avoiding it. I am a strong believer that if you can dream it, you can achieve it. If you think it, you can become it. Your thoughts become a reality and therefore you must be careful what you think about. Negative thoughts can become a reality too! On a positive note, if you can visualise your goals, where you want to be and when, and persevere through the pain, your thoughts will become a reality. Trust me. There is a difference between accepting failure and being a failure. Failing at something is acceptable, accepting your failure is not.

How it started

I feel fortunate that I have been exposed to many people who have displayed a winning mind-set. They have inspired and mentored me, often without me even knowing it; I expect you have too but may not have realised it at the time. A mentor will give you a competitive edge and help create a desire for action. I wasn't a natural athlete; everything seemed to be difficult both academically and physically for me. I was tormented for being 'podgy' at school right up until I was 15. Luckily I had a mentor who taught me the difference between winning and losing; whilst pushing me and advising me, he was also extremely supportive and listened to my problems. He always had time and would go out of his way to help me with any challenges I was facing, wanting absolutely nothing in return. He inspired me to go further than I thought possible and taught me the importance of work ethic. We all need someone like this in our life – a mentor, a coach, a mother/father figure who can guide us, challenge us, inspire us to go further.

Hugh 'Jock' Munn was all of the above, without him this book may never have been written. Many of my experiences and successes are a result of the time Jock gave me during my adolescent years, a particularly transitional time for anyone.

My father died when I was 16 and I often wonder what life would have been like had Jock not been there. I would always visit Jock before a big competition, I knew that he would give me an edge, share a few words with me that would be just enough to fill me with confidence that I often lacked in my teenage years. Jock Munn sadly passed away on 8th October 2012. Many will miss Jock – not only did he make a difference to my life but to the lives of many others. I will always hear his voice in my head when I think I have nothing left in me. I hear him telling me there is always one more rep in the gym, I can always push harder, aim higher and do more. Today I hope that I can inspire people half as much as Jock did me. Perhaps one day someone will dedicate a book to you for the difference you have made to his or her life?

Today I am developing as a coach and will continue to do so throughout my life. If you want to improve your own leadership ability, start by coaching someone – experience is the best way to learn. Even if you don't consider yourself to be a great coach, you will still add value. Find yourself a coach or a mentor; being coached is also a great way to develop the skill of coaching and will help you get to wherever you need to get to faster. I have a coach; my coach is as integral to my business as my accountant.

Like most people in my industry, I studied psychology. Sports psychology has always interested me, and was something Jock and I shared an enthusiasm for. After one of our insane training sessions in his garage, I was explaining to him how I was argumentative and that I was getting angry and frustrated with my teammates. I was 18 years old and it seemed to be getting the better of me, something I couldn't control. Jock also had a reputation during his semi-professional football career for being hot-tempered or getting the 'red mist' to the point of legendary status. He gave me a book that had helped him called *How to Win Friends and Influence People* by Dale

Carnegie (1936). It is essentially a book on common sense and had a profound impact on me at the age of 18. I found it simple to read and super easy to apply. However, the book that really influenced my performance was another by Carnegie called *Stop Worrying and Start Living* which was published in 1948. I read the book in 1997, I passed it on to a friend once I had read it, and I have never picked it up again since, although I do believe it has been much of the inspiration behind my philosophy on embracing failure.

As a result of reading the books, both my performance and the relationships on the team improved. I had learned from the book that people have a point of view. The brain of an 18-year-old finds this very difficult to comprehend. My prefrontal cortex had effectively broken down; this is the part of the brain that is effective in decision-making and seeing things from another's perspective. My emotional centre, the limbic system, which we will talk about in more detail in Part Three, had taken over and I had no rational thought; my only options were to fight or run away. This is common during adolescence. If you're a parent of a teenager, coaching a team of teenagers, or a managing anyone aged 16 to 22 in business, don't take it personally when they argue back or appear cocky. Their brain simply hasn't developed enough to maintain a mature level of communication, they will only see the mist and trying to provide wise solutions in these situations is a waste of time.

I had made a conscious effort to stop arguing with teammates or at least reduced it. There is nothing wrong with embracing a little conflict, it is what great teams do. Reading those two books launched my thirst for knowledge on the subject of psychology. Having not read a single book at school apart from *The BFG* by Roald Dahl, I had become obsessed with reading. I would read anything to do with philosophy, psychology and business that would give me insight into how I could improve my personal performance in sport, life and my career.

In recent years the focus of my study has been on the brain and the application of neuroscience to enhance leadership and team performance. The study of neuroscience is providing valid scientific insight into cognitive behaviour and this insight will help you manage your behaviour more effectively. There has, however, been a recent increase in popularising neuroscience, with coined phrases such as NeuroLeadership, NeuroCoaching and NeuroSelling. I'm not against this and anything that promotes performance improvement can only be a good thing, although I am making no attempt to popularise neuroscience other than to back up the theories I am sharing with you with some academic rigour.

I must also add that I'm not a neuroscientist and I am very grateful to Dr Colin Wallace and the Centre for Applied Neuroscience for their support. The Centre is a non-profit-making, interdisciplinary, membership organisation devoted to education, involving the latest advances in brain research. It is also dedicated to raising awareness of the need for interaction between individuals and research groups involved in the application of the neurosciences. In particular, it focuses on research and discoveries that enhance understanding of the neural bases of human behaviour.

Much of what I have learned and taught others has been intuitive, based on my own experiences in playing hockey and working in sales and coaching roles. I have come to the conclusion that the psychology community, with its roots in philosophy and extensive research, has 'described' behaviour and neuroscience is supporting the research by 'explaining' it at a scientific level. Understanding the function of your brain will give you insights into why you do the things that you do and help you develop techniques for managing behaviour more effectively. My aim has been to find the balance between theory and application and therefore I have kept the neuroscience element as simple and easy to understand as possible.

CHAPTER 2

CREATING WINNING MIND-SETS

Creating Winning Mind-sets

Winning Mindset Consulting's first client back in 2008 was a company based in Canary Wharf, London that specialised in training day traders. They approached me about my philosophy on the winning mind-set and asked if I could come in and run workshops. Whilst they were experts in teaching traders the fundamental aspects of trading, they wanted someone to help with the psychological challenges. Trading, and particularly day trading, is extremely stressful, it involves huge amounts of mental toughness, a strong nerve and an appetite for risk. Day traders can become very emotional and stressed. The constant swing of dopamine when trading is going well, followed by the rush of cortisol and adrenaline when results are bad, causes a volatile and turbulent set of emotions – what I refer to later in the book as the 'emotional roller coaster'. The aim was to help traders avoid the emotional roller coaster during crisis situations and learn to accept the failures that come their way. Just like in sport, failure is part of the process, it needs to be embraced, and trading was no exception to this.

The workshop lasted four hours; it was called 'A Winning Mind-set for Traders' and it emphasised the link between sports performance and trading performance, particularly around staying in the zone. I ran a workshop every month at Canary Wharf for aspiring traders over a two-year period. During that time, a range of personalities participated in the workshops but they appeared to have one thing in common: they wanted to make money, although when I probed deeper below the surface there were other reasons for making money, such as freedom, recognition, personal development, time with their family etc. However, at the core was a desired future state that was propelling them to want more than they already had and they believed that a career in trading would get them there. For example, when I asked them what does a day look like in 18 months to five years when they become successful traders, they would respond with: "I'll have two houses, one in Florida and one in Italy" or "I will ski in the morning and trade in the afternoon when the market opens" and "I'll be driving an Aston Martin." These tended to be mainly materialistic items and much more than they already had in reality. I have no problem with this – if it drives them to succeed and provides purpose in their lives then why not?

Going from Good to Great

In 2010 I was working on a community project for charity in London that specialises in helping the homeless and getting them back into work. My role was to deliver a similar workshop to the one for traders to a group of 20 homeless people, which we simply called 'Winning Mind-set'.

One of the exercises that I used and still use today is called 'Pain versus Pleasure'. It had the aim to inspire the group of individuals to take action towards pleasure (their vision) and move away from the pain they were currently in. I now simply call it 'Good to Great' and apart from a potential lawsuit with Jim Collins, author of *Good to Great,* I think it is a better name for the exercise. However, to move from good to great may involve change which can be a painful experience.

At the beginning of the exercise I ask participants to describe on post-it notes how they will feel when they achieve their vision; I ask them to describe what they will see and hear when the vision is a reality, and then stick the notes up at one end of the room. At the other end of the room I ask them to do the same but this time I ask them to describe what life will be like if nothing changes. The aim of this is to create urgency to move away from the current state towards their future goals. When I read out some of the descriptions on the post-its, I realised that I had made a serious error.

As I read the notes I could feel myself becoming emotional, something I had not anticipated or prepared for. The notes said things like 'kill myself', 'buy a gun' and 'jump off a cliff'. At the other end of the room I was expecting to read similar goals to the traders such as 'five-bedroom house', 'successful career' or 'new car'. The first one I read said 'a cleaning job'; I asked the group "Who wrote 'cleaning job'?" A man responded quietly with a large smile "Me." I said "It is great that you are clear on what you want; tell me, what are you doing currently?" He responded with "A cleaning job." I continued naively: "OK, so what will this cleaning job be like in the future?" He replied contently "The same one I have now" and again putting my own agenda on to him, I said "Don't you want more?" He said that his cleaning job was so precious to him and he was so grateful that he could support his family that the prospect of not having the cleaning job was unthinkable.

It was a serious lesson for me, and now I am very careful with whoever I work with, whether it is a charity or a group of highly paid executives. I have learned to never have an agenda. Many leaders have an agenda; they become too focused on the goals they want to achieve, with their own personality bias, and ignore any contribution from their team. A COO once said to me when reviewing a proposal I had sent: "Andrew, I don't want their involvement in the strategy, if these people have knowledge of what's going on around here they will become dangerous." On another occasion, a director of a learning and development function at a global organisation said to me that as long as she knew what her individual team members were doing in isolation and hitting their objectives, they didn't need to know what each other was doing. Really? This type of coercive 'command and control' style will always end in loss of control.

How can an engaged, autonomous and strategically aligned team be dangerous? This is not dangerous, this is a high-performance culture. Please don't let your ego get in the way and make the same mistake – it will be detrimental to you and your team's future performance.

Now you may think that the 'Good to Great' exercise is simple and that everyone will move quickly from one side of the room to the other. It is a surprisingly challenging exercise and often creates inertia within the group, particularly when the exercise is facilitated with a team. Participants find it very difficult to move across, especially when I ask them to consider what may be obstructing them, what the barriers are etc. When I use this with senior management teams it can take up to two hours to make it to the other side of the room. The exercise creates much debate and encourages them to talk about the 'elephant in the room' and get things out in the open. Transparency and openness is crucial for achieving a high-performing team. It is essential to embrace this type of conflict when moving towards becoming a great team. At an individual level it is also important to identify with what will get in your way. It is often our own way of thinking, as I discovered with the charity as described above.

As I continued to facilitate, I was fascinated to see how engaged they became. What I observed initially was paralysis caused by fear of failure. They appeared to be frozen to the spot and refused to cross the room, even to take a single step. I asked them what they could see that was stopping them from walking across. One lady said "A blob, I see a blob on the floor in front of me." "Describe the blob to me," I responded. She looked down curiously, with her hand on her chin. She paused for a while and then said softly as if she had had a eureka moment "It's me, I see me." "What are you going to do?" I asked. She stood still for a while. Nervously she said "I want to step over but I'm scared." A man at the back said "Let's use the chairs to build a bridge!" The entire group was getting excited by the idea of building a bridge to get over the barrier as if they were all experiencing the same thing. After 45 minutes the group eventually made it to the other side with a sense of achievement and clarity. It was an emotional moment for the group and had a very humbling effect on me.

The main barrier preventing us from moving towards our goal, as with the woman above, is in fact ourselves. It is our conscious voice, i.e. the mind, and your ability to manage your thoughts and feelings is the difference between success and failure, winning and losing. You have a choice – don't let your way of thinking hold you back.

Manage the Gap

The gap between what you have and what you want will determine how satisfied you are. For example, the cleaner I mentioned earlier was happy with his job and his goal was to maintain what he had. It is still a goal even though it was the same as his current position, whereas with the traders, the gap was much bigger.

It is has been proven that the gap between what we have and what we don't have is what makes us happy. When you are about to win or achieve something, your brain will experience a rush of dopamine. Dopamine is a neurotransmitter that helps control your brain's reward and pleasure centres. The chemical also helps you regulate movement and emotional responses, and it enables you not only to see rewards, but also to take action to move towards them. The presence of dopamine is also associated with risk-taking and excitement. This suggests that motivation doesn't come from achieving the goal; it comes from the anticipation of achieving the goal. For example, you don't often see an Olympic gold medallist jump around on the podium with joy; they actually appear to be more relaxed, relieved and emotional. This is because it is the anticipation of achieving success that is really driving them. When an athlete reminisces over the pain they went through to achieve their goal, they often recall it was the best part of their career. This might explain why many athletes suffer with depression when they retire, because they lose their purpose and drive.

Other examples are booking a holiday, opening a present or shopping. It is the process of making the booking or the unwrapping of a present that gets us excited, not necessarily the outcome. Often the holiday is an anticlimax, the present doesn't meet expectations and once the shopping experience is over it is followed by a low. The constant need for dopamine can result in addictive behaviour and needs to be managed carefully. There is a theory that this type of behaviour contributed to the financial meltdown of 2008, namely that a form of addiction to the 'pleasure' of profit had the effect of overriding the need for careful risk management.

Whilst accomplishing a goal is rewarding, staying motivated actually comes from being satisfied with what you are 'doing' not from what you have 'done'. Therefore how you manage the gap between what you have and what you don't have is key to your well-being and developing the right mind-set for success.

Pain is the best part

As mentioned before, when you are moving from good to great you and your team may experience pain. Change is painful, both physically and emotionally. We are surrounded by change. There is more change today than ever. Just when you thought you had bought the latest piece of technology, a friend is showing off a newer version. An organisation may be making changes to its processes, culture, perhaps even making redundancies, which can trigger anxiety, stress and uncertainty.

Neuroscience research has shown that receptors in the brain that respond to physical pain are the same receptors that respond to emotional change, proving that change is physically painful. Someone may find themselves in a dysfunctional relationship, they know it is not healthy for them, but the pain of leaving that person may be worse than the pain they are already in, so they avoid the pain and find comfort in the pain where they are.

Regardless of the type of change, individuals will suffer varying degrees of pain during change. Any type of change that may cause someone to experience the grieving process requires a particular type of support. If someone went to see a therapist to aid them with their grieving process, it is unlikely that the therapist would ignore it, or ask them to 'pull their socks up and get on with their job'. An alternative softer approach is required from leadership when employees are experiencing painful change. I'm not suggesting that you become a therapist, far from it, but it does highlight the importance of an emotional approach when dealing with change.

Change can be very fast, too fast for some people. In business there is constant change and this can cause anxiety in employees if they feel they cannot keep up with the pace. Nearly half of long-term absences are caused by stress and it is costing the economy billions. You are either someone who embraces change and enjoys the variety, perhaps you're happy to make a few mistakes along the way and learn from them. Or you are someone who won't even attempt to change until you are sure you can deal with it and therefore prefer a clear framework and certainty.

Athletes go through change during their careers. They have to learn to adapt to new rules and regulations. They are given new equipment designed to enhance their performance; in some cases it may have a detrimental effect on performance in the short term. Very often an athlete will have to change their technique to reach their desired outcome. For example, a golfer may have to change her swing to improve her performance. Initially the golfer's performance will drop, she will get worse at playing golf. Unfortunately, there is no fairy dust to sprinkle over the golfer that will advance her there quicker. The golfer will have to go through the pain of losing matches, failing to achieve the results she was achieving before. The golfer will find it very challenging and may even consider going back to her comfort zone. She may find pleasure in the pain of being in that old place again, returning to her old style and giving up on her goal. The only way you will move from good to great is by persevering through the pain performance and achieving better results. It is a choice that the golfer will have to make around her behaviour.

Jessica Ennis is a great example of an athlete who has been forced to change due to injury. Ennis's foot injury meant she had to change her take-off leg in the long jump from right to left in 2009. This is like trying to learn to write with your other hand! Three years later she was on the podium at the 2012 Olympics with a gold medal round her neck.

Another good example of an athlete managing change is Ashley Jackson who represented Team Great Britain at field hockey at the Athens, Beijing and London Olympics. Not a lot of people know that Jackson started out life as an ice hockey player until turning his hand to field hockey. He had the potential to play professionally on the ice; furthermore, he plays ice hockey left-handed and field hockey right-handed – and he is frustratingly great at both. Due to the fact that field hockey is only played right-handed, Ashley had to teach himself to play field hockey the opposite way to how he had grown up playing ice hockey. It takes drive and passion to make this type of transition. He has achieved huge success and he is one of most mentally tough athletes I have had the pleasure to work with.

In the mid-1980s, Nick Faldo famously decided to take action and change his technique to make himself a better player. The British golfer decided to change his swing. With the help of coach David Leadbetter, Faldo's swing became more efficient and he accomplished his goal. He hit 1,500 practice balls a day. The practising paid off and in 1989 he won his second major tournament, the Masters. Faldo went on to win a number of other tournaments in 1989, including the Volvo PGA Championship and the Dunhill British Masters. Had he not made the brave decision and taken the risk to make the changes to his swing, he may never have won those competitions.

Leaders and teams will experience change at some point. Their ability to manage change, embrace the unknown and persevere through the pain will eventually help them achieve their goals. Pain may be in the form of failures and challenges and these failures are great opportunities to learn. When they arrive at their destination, they will be stronger than ever.
There is no direct route to a better future state. You may have to sacrifice things in your life that are important to you in order to achieve your goals. This could be your relationships, hobbies and social life. In some cases it could even be your ego. You may find that moving away from your current state means change. If you avoid going through this process then you are unlikely to reach your full potential. Take a risk and enjoy what you learn from it.

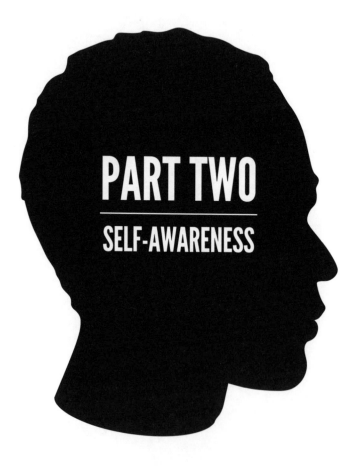

PART TWO

SELF-AWARENESS

CHAPTER 3

GET TO KNOW YOU

"Your visions will become clear only when you can look into your own heart. Who looks outside, dreams; who looks inside, awakes."
Carl Jung

As discussed earlier, developing self-awareness is essential for developing a winning mind-set. There are a number of models and theories on leadership, but a key competency is self-awareness. A lack of self-awareness will seriously inhibit your ability to gain a competitive advantage.

In this part of the book we will take a closer look at behaviour and motivation. By the end of this section you will have identified with your own behavioural preference and leadership style, what motivates you and the importance of being passionate about what you do. I recommend a pen and paper for this part, as you may want to make some notes.

There is a clear distinction between personality and behaviour, as described by Robin Stuart-Kotze in his book simply named *Performance: The Secrets of Successful Behaviour* (2006). "Personality is who you are and behaviour is what you do." Behaviour drives performance, you may have all the skills and knowledge in the world but if you don't have the right set of behaviours in place all your talent will be wasted. Behaviour is what you do, not who you are. Therefore, whatever your personality type is you can still flex, change and adapt your behaviour. By doing so, in time you will create new habits that are going to help you achieve your goals.

It is important to know what your own preference for doing things is, so that you can increase your ability to work with others and get the best out them; by doing so you will also learn how to get the best out of you. Whilst there will be things that you know about yourself that others don't, there will also be things that others know about you that you don't know about yourself. These are often referred to as behavioural 'blind spots'. Blind spots are an opportunity for improving performance; unfortunately, many people choose to avoid acknowledging their blind spots due to their ego. They cannot accept that they have developmental areas and pretend that they are super human beings who can never be seen doing anything wrong. The problem here is that they are unaware of the 'blind spot' whilst those around them can clearly see it. These people become less open to accepting feedback and never award themselves with the opportunity to improve their performance.

Being open to feedback may cause you to feel vulnerable. You may be concerned with what people think of you. You may also worry about being a failure or being seen as a failure. Perhaps you have been promoted into a role or playing in a position where people have high expectations of you and you can't bring yourself to ask for help. You may feel that it will be perceived as a sign of weakness. Actually it takes more bravery to ask for help than it does to pretend that everything is perfectly fine. Becoming comfortable with feeling vulnerable is a source of enlightenment that will free you from the chains of perfection and the fear of failure.

Neuroscience of Leadership

Becoming more self-aware will also help you to create a holistic strategy for both you and your team. It will ensure that your preference towards how you like things to be done won't interfere and cause a bias towards how you achieve your personal and team goals. A useful way to identify with your behavioural preference is to complete a psychometric questionnaire. There are hundreds of tools on the market – some are plausible and some very poor. There are three which I use including Hogan, Risk-Type Compass and *PRISM* Brain Mapping. They can be used in business, enabling you to understand yourself and others better, thus creating a dynamic and high-performing team.

First, let's understand what is determining your behaviour at a brain science level. During the last 15 years we have learned more about the brain than in our entire existence and we are still only touching the surface. Whilst psychology has been able to identify with personality and behavioural types, neuroscience is explaining what is happening in a physiological way. Neuroscience research has shown that there are links between behaviour and the two hemispheres of the brain. To keep things simple I have described the behaviours in four groups as seen below.

What type of leader are you?

The Centre for Applied Neuroscience has successfully created four groups to describe different types of leadership behaviour. The research is based on studies that link behaviour with the balance of chemicals and hormones in the brain. It is likely that you will recognise yourself in all of them; however, you will have an overriding preference or bias towards how you like to do things based on the balance of chemicals and hormones in your brain, which will influence how you communicate with others and your approach to creating a strategy for your team. Having knowledge of your preference is an integral component of the 'Get Your House in Order' strategy model which I will introduce in Part Four. See which one you recognise yourself in.

The Results-Driven Leader

If you have this preference you will have a focus on results, which is associated with the left hemisphere of the brain. You will be turned on by the opportunity to accept challenges, create action and obtain results. You are driven to overcome opposition in order to accomplish goals. If someone tells you something cannot be achieved, you will set out to prove him or her wrong. You are quick to seize opportunities that allow you to assume control of your environment. Tell you that there will be rewards to recognise those who produce the most in the least amount of time and there is no doubt you will be first to achieve top results. You will pursue your goals. You may sometimes view the opinions of others as obstacles rather than helpful suggestions. You possess an unusual ability to thrive in negative environments. Your motto tends to be: 'Get it done and don't make excuses'.

The Process-Driven Leader

If you have this preference you will have a focus on process, which is associated with the left hemisphere of the brain. You are motivated not just by results but also by quality results. You tend to be low-key, factual and extremely accurate. You are at your best when a job needs to be done with precision. You set high standards for yourself and others, and expect everyone to comply, always with the same high standards. Part of your drive for quality, accuracy and order is derived from your strong desire for a structured environment. You prefer a logical, step-by-step approach to tasks. For you, even life itself should proceed along a predictable path. You believe in yourself, your capabilities and your intellectual skills. You pride yourself on your ability to solve complex problems – the more complex the better. Your motto is: "I can't move on until I get it right".

The Culture-Driven Leader

If you have this preference you are what I call the 'Culture-Driven Leader'. You will have a focus on creating a harmonious culture, which is associated with the right hemisphere of the brain. You are a team player who has a desire to please and maintain stability in a group, even if it means sacrificing your own personal goals. You are driven by harmony, agreement and loyalty. You prefer to keep things as they are and provide a stabilising influence by the consistent way in which you go about your day-to-day work. You do well in handling routine matters. Change, therefore, is unwelcome. If you work in a friendly, low-stress and slow-paced work environment, there is no doubt that you will be a happy, committed worker who will do the best to please your bosses and colleagues, and lend a helping hand along the way. Your motto tends to be: "Don't rock the boat".

The Image-Driven Leader

If you have this type of preference you are what I call the 'Image-Driven Leader'. A focus on image and external perception is associated with the right hemisphere of the brain. Your personal image and branding is important to you. You have a strong ability to persuade others to agree with you. You need to have the opportunity to express your ideas and opinions. This helps you to achieve social recognition. If you are told that a new, improved method is needed, you will jump at the opportunity to invent it. If asked to use your creative skills, you will provide unlimited possibilities, and with such energetic enthusiasm that others will be drawn into your dreams along with you. You will want to have the freedom to do things your way, and you will produce ingenious results. Spontaneous by nature, your motto tends to be: "Ready, aim, fire!"

Know your style

Take your time to reflect on what you think your preferred style is, although you may recognise yourself in all four, one will manifest itself, particularly when you are under pressure. Knowing your style also plays a key role when devising a strategy ensuring you use a 'whole brain approach' as described in part four.

Adapting your style

Neuroscience research shows that there is no 'single self' to be found in the human brain. Each person is made up of several, sometimes conflicting, behaviour preferences rather than a single unchanging personality. You may display entirely different behaviours at times: sometimes you will be talkative and sometimes withdrawn; sometimes cooperative and sometimes quarrelsome; sometimes relaxed and sometimes anxious. For example, you will have noticed that you behave and feel very differently when you are on holiday, or when you are with one set of friends as opposed to another, or when you are with family rather than strangers.

To be successful in flexing your preferential behaviour you will require a strong ability to self-regulate your emotions. This will enhance your clarity of judgement and the ability to shift your style when necessary. Daniel Goleman describes the ability to be self-aware as a key competency for being 'emotionally intelligent'. Emotional Intelligence is a term that is often thrown around the leadership development arena. Emotional Intelligence can be developed; as well as being self-aware it is also important to be socially aware and to understand other people's preference and how to get the best out of them. For example, you would need to deliver a message differently to someone who prefers a high-level overview than you would to someone who is meticulous and has a high attention to detail.

Change is painful and any type of behavioural change may feel clunky and awkward. Some of your behaviours will be hard-wired; fortunately for you, your brain has elasticity, and it can create new neural pathways, learn new ways of doing things and develop new habits. Until 20 years ago, it was believed that change was only for young people and that the brain started to deteriorate and was not able to continue developing into old age. Due to recent studies in neuroscience, we now know this not to be the case.

Whether you are leading change, starting a business or taking your team to the championships, you'll require the ability to flex your communication style to meet the needs of every individual on your team. Everyone is unique and requires unique attention. They will have different standards, motives, values and most importantly they will offer you different strengths. It is easy for a leader to dismiss a person's strengths if they clash with their own preference. It is common to want to work with people most like us, but how does that add value to the team? To create a high-performance team requires input from all types of preferences.

Good facilitation skills, patience and trust are required to engage your team and inspire them towards a vision. This will help you share decision-making, dynamism and synergy amongst your team. You will need to adopt a flexible approach and demonstrate or acquire the ability to flex your style depending on the situation, whilst simultaneously remaining aligned to your personal values. However, you may find that your values change over time, such as becoming a selfless leader, less ego driven; this type of change will manifest itself in behaviour, and therefore inspiring leadership. You may need to learn new behaviours, adopt strengths that you see in others, identify strengths in people who can add value, perhaps where you can't. I am certain that I have learned new positive behaviours from members on my team.

In theory, all behaviours can be learned. Due to research into neuroscience, we know that the brain is malleable, organic and forever changing. But in the short term no one person is up to developing all the different preferences overnight, no matter what you think or what your superior expects from you. Even if you wanted to, your brain simply isn't that malleable! I have no problem with you stretching yourself and developing yourself in other areas – I actively encourage it. However, as Dr Carl Jung who coined the phrase "falsification of type" suggests, people are more effective and happier when they are working within their own preference. When you are working beyond your comfort zone and spend too much time stretching yourself, it can lead to poor health and exhaustion. You will use a hundred times more oxygen and glucose when working under stress. I am a massive advocate of stretching ourselves and exceeding our own expectations, but spending too much time in this space is not a good thing. Utilise all the resources you have available, don't dismiss talent simply because the behaviour clashes with yours.

Copy them and do it better!

We have all met people that we aspire to be, people we look up to and try to be like. I have a confession to make: my sports career was based on the fact that I observed players who were better than me, copied their style and behaviour and tried to do it better. I still do it today when I play; the only difference is that my inspiration comes from players who are younger than me now!

From the moment you were born you learned to model behaviour. Parents teach their children all the time through role-model behaviour. Sometimes they do not know they are doing it. A new-born child will have 100 billion neurons in their brain which are ready to aid their growth and development. The early overproduction of neurons and neural networks guarantees that the young brain will be capable of adapting to virtually any new environment into which the child is born. Parents teach their children whenever the children are watching. Children see what the parents do. They learn from parents' words and actions. They learn what ways of behaving are good and what ways are not good by watching parents striking the balance between nurture and nature. The best way for parents to help their children develop good behaviour is by exhibiting the behaviours themselves – and leadership is no exception.

Your brain has developed since being in your mother's womb and will continue to develop throughout your life. Your brain weighed about 350 grams at birth and as an adult between 1,300-1,500 grams. Your brain has gone through significant changes, particularly between the ages of one to ten years. At the age of six months it will have grown to 50% the weight of an adult brain, 60% at 18 months, 75% at two and half years and 95% of your adult weight at age ten. Recent research has shown that an adult brain also makes dramatic changes between the ages of 30-70, destroying any traditional beliefs about brain development. All the time you are developing new behaviours, learning new tasks such as languages or playing a musical instrument for example, you will continue to grow neural pathways in your brain. This scientific insight provides an amazing opportunity for development and performance improvement.

As an adult you can adopt the behaviour of those you admire and respect, who conduct themselves in a way that inspires you. There is no harm in imitating people who are good at what they do. Why try and reinvent the wheel? If it works, copy it and do it better.

The key to modelling behaviour is remaining authentic to who you are, i.e. your personality, who you are and what you value in life. Your personality manifests itself as behaviour and therefore is easier to adapt and change depending on the situation and environment. An analogy that is often cited is an iceberg used to illustrate Freud's structure of the human mind. The mind is likened to an iceberg – only the tip of an iceberg, or the mind, is visible. This is our conscious awareness or seen behaviour. Just under the sea level is our unconscious. The vast bulk of the iceberg or mind is hidden from view. We are unaware of it. Our unconscious contains our instincts, motivations and fears. It is where both genetic and long-forgotten memories of personality-forming experiences are held.

The mind can consciously change the way we behave, but the unconscious can override this when under pressure and we behave instinctively or irrationally, which we will go into in more detail in Part Three when we explore staying in the zone. The key to modelling behaviour is to firstly model good behaviour. Sounds obvious, but I have seen many young athletes lose their way due to modelling themselves on the wrong people who at first may appear to have great talent, but lack the appropriate behaviours required for high performance. Also you can assimilate the best behaviours from several people. As a young athlete I wanted to acquire the work ethic, skills and aptitude of all the best players; no one single player seemed to have them all. I made it my aim to have them all. By the way, it is still a work in progress even as a veteran!

I have experienced the power of this first-hand when I moved to work for a FTSE 100 media sales company. Previously I had always worked in the sports industry in some form or another. I spent three years working for a ski company as a sales and marketing manager. I'd had a fantastic time, I met great people, and I skied in Italy, France, Austria and California, and I got paid for it. Despite the great times, the ski industry is very much a lifestyle industry and I felt the time had come to gain some corporate experience. Apart from the role with the ski company, I had only worked in retail and ran my own sports development business helping get young people into sport. It still exists today, although it has become more of a labour of love than a business.

So I ditched the skis and bought myself a suit. I met with a recruitment agency, they set me up with an interview with the media sales company, and two months later I started life as a field sales consultant selling advertising. On my first day, dressed in a cheap suit, I received a laptop, a Ford Focus and a mobile phone. It was a far cry from driving a van, wearing baggy jeans and beanie hat. It was also quite a shift from having a sales meeting in the Alps to discussing directory advertising in the plumbing classification, but I was happy to give it go for six months and see what happened.

There were several field sales levels at the media sales company and the natural next step for me was to become an account executive. The main difference between the two roles was the size of the accounts being dealt with. The thing I noticed the most was the quality of the suits that the account executives wore, perhaps because I had experience working in the rag trade and had an eye for this type of thing. Having said that, this was the first role where I had ever had to wear a suit. Account executives looked dapper: nice suits, shiny expensive shoes, nicely knotted ties – nothing like my £99 suit and £15 shirts (£40 for three). After six months in the role it was clear to me that I wanted to be an account executive, but I would have to change the way I worked and looked.

I have always believed that if you look good you feel good. So with the commission I had made I decided to make an investment in myself. I bought myself a nice suit and better shoes; I bought a leather briefcase rather than using the standard issue. I spoke to account executives, building rapport and learning from them; I would ask if I could shadow them for a day and observe what they did. I started to imitate some of their behaviours with my own clients. I noticed how my clients were taking me more seriously, my credibility increased, immediately my confidence grew, my presence improved in the office and my performance shot through the roof. After just 12 months in the job I got an interview for an account executive role. I'll never forget the regional manager smiling at me at the end of the interview and saying: "The thing is, Andrew, your results are good but you also look the part."

The Behaviour Modelling Cycle

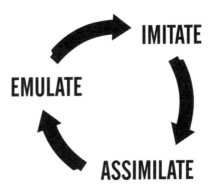

There are three steps in the Behaviour Modelling Cycle. Firstly **imitate** the best. When I got my job as an account executive I made sure I sat opposite Bill Sidebottom (name has been changed to protect the innocent – well kind of innocent). He had consistently been the best sales executive for 25 years, he had the long service watch, the Mercedes car, the 25-year ring, and he had plenty of stories. I wanted to know what his recipe for success was. I would listen to him making prospect calls, talking to clients, how he booked in meetings with difficult customers etc. He had what I lacked, he was extremely results driven and always kept the end result in mind, which was an important part of closing the deal. It was an area of development for me. Whilst Bill was good at certain things, there were also a number of ways in which he worked that disconnected with my values, which I did not take on and looked elsewhere for more ethical consultants who had demonstrated behaviours that I could connect with.

The next step is to **assimilate** the behaviours: what are the skills and behaviours you have noticed about the person, what are they doing differently? What do you like and dislike? Which ones are you going to adopt? In Bill's case I wanted to assimilate his ability to close the sale. Whilst my strengths are building rapport, developing strong relationships with my clients, unlike Bill closing didn't come naturally to me. I was avoiding the potential conflict and the negotiation that were a part of closing sales with the larger accounts I was working with. As I'm sure you are aware, to be a top performer in sales, embracing conflict and negotiation are essential to achieving success. In the words of my manager, which seemed appropriate at the time: "You need to grow bigger balls." So I did, I started to pitch big, I started to relish the art of negotiation, I used my strengths at building rapport to get negotiation down to a fine art. I embraced failure by asking myself what is the worst that can happen, they may say no, and so what if they do? I became more relaxed about the whole process and my performance improved.

The next step in the cycle is to **emulate** those skills and behaviours, copy them and do it better! I knew I could build stronger relationships than Bill, that was my key strength and, as we discussed earlier, a strengths-focused approach will achieve more in the long run. I built loyalty with my customers, and now with my new found ability to close more effectively, I was on my way to becoming a better sales person. Over time, closing became a habit rather than a conscious choice. Through practice I had created new neural pathways in my brain. My new behaviours became subconscious and allowed my conscious mind to focus attention on developing new behaviours and therefore start the cycle over again.

Those with a winning mind-set focus on continuous performance improvement, they are thinking ahead, being proactive. When I hear people say "if isn't broken then don't fix it" I think to myself, "so are you going to wait for it to break and then fix it?" Surely that will be too late?

Athletes are told to 'keep drinking water, don't wait until you're thirsty because it'll be too late, keep topping up, keep sipping'. You will have to do the same in the workplace and in life: keep topping up, keep learning, don't leave it until it breaks because it'll be too late, there is no room for complacency when developing a winning mind-set. The game is always tied; even when you are three goals up, keep striving, keep moving forward, keep pushing harder, you'll only ever live up to your expectations, so set them high.

CHAPTER 4

MOTIVATION

What is Motivation?

In this chapter we are going to explore your strengths, motivations and the importance of being passionate about what you do. I am also going to share with you what prompted me to take up street hockey at age nine and how it evolved. I have utilised my passion for sport to stay motivated in everything I do by identifying with what truly motivates me. By the end of this chapter you will start to do the same. Motivation is often top of the agenda when it comes to creating high-performance teams. Whenever I start a management training programme I always ask delegates what they want to take away from the training. The response is usually "How do I motivate my team members?" Leaders, coaches and managers alike want to find ways to motivate their people. You will find what drives you to succeed may be very different from your peers and your team members. A friend of mine has been planning his exit strategy from investment banking for the last five years. He doesn't want to leave until he has paid the mortgage on his £1.2 million house. What is motivating him to stay in a job that he doesn't like? Is it simply money or is there something more intrinsic driving him to stay that perhaps he is unaware of? This leads me to consider what the motivation is for a chosen career or even hobby. It is widely accepted that a career for life is rare. Not only are people switching jobs, they are changing their career entirely and this comes at a cost. Since I moved from a sales career into management consulting in 2007 I have invested over £30,000 in my own development, not to mention the pay cut I took when I made the transition. I certainly wasn't doing it for the money back then; what I can say now though is that I have no intention to retire ever. I love my job too much and hope I can work until my final breath and go out in style like Tommy Cooper.

If you are managing or coaching a team and you want to create a high-performance culture, don't fall into the trap of trying to create perfect human beings, it won't work. Also remember that people are motivated in different ways. Even if you have similar personalities, it is likely they are driven to succeed for different reasons from yours; even if they do say they're doing it for the money, what is driving them to make money may be entirely different.

I made this mistake when I became a sales manager for the media sales company. I had been successful as a consultant and typically, as in all meritocratic cultures, I got promoted into a manager's role. I was very excited about the amazing things I was going to do with the team. I had acquired the lowest performing team in the division and I knew I could get us to the top. My plan seemed logical and rational. I wanted to get my team members to work in the same way I did, I was a top performer and I knew what worked. I spent time with the under-performers with the aim to get them to the same level as the top performers in the team and I believed we would see a difference within six months.

The results were quite clear. My under-performers didn't change their behaviour; my focus was on their skills which made them feel scrutinised and picked on, they became even more demotivated and performance dropped further. My top performers felt neglected and my relationship broke down with them. With my team members who weren't top performers but were consistently hitting target, their performance also dropped. They were annoyed with me for making them work in a particular way just because it worked for me and it is fair to say that after six months I still had the lowest performing team in the division. I never asked the questions, we didn't establish a team purpose or goal, there was no plan or process in place and, most importantly, we didn't discuss the type of behaviours required for success.

I have learned from the experience and there are things that I just don't do today. It still amazes me though when I see experienced managers trying to force their own style of management onto others; they also tend to recruit people who are similar to them. They have a bias towards behaviours like their own, results-driven leaders recruit results-driven people etc. In the short term, the relationship will be easier, but the team will lack dynamism. They try so hard to motivate their team with their own motivations. For me this is the fundamental difference between motivation and inspiration. If you want to motivate someone you need to know what gets him or her out of bed in the morning and what will drive him or her. Identify with what they are passionate about, what motivates and drives them. There will always be people who you clash with or potentially want to avoid, it is human nature, but you will have to find a way to inspire action. The best way to do this is through utilising their strengths and what motivates them.

You don't need to be loud and charismatic to inspire a group towards a goal; you just need the confidence to have the conversation and ask the questions. As with coaching, a key skill when engaging your team is the quality of the question. Questioning techniques are at the heart of identifying strengths and motivations and facilitating a high-performance team. Asking open questions such as: "What do you like best about your job? What would make your job more satisfying? What are your aspirations for the future? What gets you out of bed in the morning?" Have the confidence to probe further, asking: "What else? Tell me more... Explain what you mean by that. Describe it to me." The answers will be limited if you ask any questions starting with "Is there?" or "Do you?" or "Can you?" and the conversation will be less rich. When their motivational needs and drivers are being met, you are more likely to get the best out of your team. It is important that you are able to draw out what each individual team member wants and what is going to motivate him or her towards the vision. Their personal vision will need to be aligned to your team vision, and if you are part of an organisation it will need to align all the way through to the corporate vision. This will create strategic alignment, engagement and passion and will ensure 'buy in' to the vision at every level.

When I joined the media advertising company I was told that I would excel in sales because of my sports background. I was puzzled at the time – although it sounded good and I nodded in response, it occurred to me that selling advertising space was entirely different to playing sport. My passion for competing in sport consumed me, it was all I thought about, and my life was designed around sport. What I ate, how I trained, my relationships, everything I did needed to fit around sport. However, over the years I have learned how to look deep inside and contextualise my passion in sport and apply it into the workplace. All athletes have skills that can be transferred into the workplace. Your strengths, motivations and passion in life are at the very core of what makes you great. Identifying with these areas will help you increase your performance and the performance of others.

The Seven Motivators of the World

The Seven Motivators of the World was an idea I developed for the 'Winning Mind-set for Traders' workshop in 2008. The model is loosely based on Maslow's Hierarchy of Needs, which apparently has now been developed into an eight-stage hierarchy of needs. I don't see the motivators as a hierarchy or as stages; they are simply needs that we all have which may vary throughout our lives. Staying motivated during difficult and challenging times is hard for anyone; it is especially hard for a trader. When things get really bad it may mean bankruptcy. This can cause a serious fear of failure and paralysis to take action.

Before working with the traders I had made the assumption that they were purely in it for the money, expecting gregarious, money-hungry nutcases, with the behaviours of a psychopath. I didn't meet one. I met a range of different personalities and behaviours. Whilst making money was top of their agenda, their motivation differed. I noticed this after about the third workshop. I would ask them what they would spend their money on. I would get answers like: "Spend more time with my family"; "Buy an Aston Martin"; "Improve my work/life balance"; and "Do a Masters degree." I would then ask more questions to gain a deeper understanding, such as: "And what does having an Aston Martin mean to you?" or "Describe to me what a good work/life balance looks and feels like for you." The answers would vary dramatically. Two people could want an Aston Martin for entirely different reasons. Therefore I cannot take the credit for the seven motivators as they were generated by their answers, not me simply making them up. Here they are in no particular order, take your time and consider which motivators resonate with you.

 **SENSE OF WELLBEING**

If you are motivated by a sense of well-being you will have a desire for contentment, satisfaction, being healthy and relaxed. It is unlikely that you will want to work in stressful environments, or if you do you will make sure it does not impact on health or work/life balance. You will avoid anything that causes you to feel anxious or unhappy. You may feel comfortable earning enough money to cover your bills and basic needs, rather than working too far outside of your comfort zone. Flexible working hours that meet your personal needs will motivate you; perhaps building in time for travel, for downtime and being healthy will increase your happiness over working hard for materialistic things.

RELATIONSHIPS

If you are motivated by relationships you will prefer to work with people rather than by yourself. You will want to stay connected and form strong relationships in life and in work. The social environment is a source of energy for you, you feed off people and their ideas. Team ethos and camaraderie is important to you. Being loyal to your team is something that you value and it is likely that you will find working alone demotivating. You welcome a connection that is not just limited to work and work assignments or projects. You value collaborating and teamwork in the workplace and you also enjoy forming close bonds outside of work.

MAKING A DIFFERENCE

You have a selfless desire to help others. You will want to change things for the better and create an environment for better living conditions. You will not be bothered by the status that it brings you. Your only concern is that other people are happier because of what you have done. You may find that humanitarian and charity work inspires you. Giving up your time to raise awareness, money and making the world a better place is something that you truly value.

RECOGNITION

Being recognised for good work will be important to you – this can be in the form of both intrinsic and extrinsic motivation. Recognition will come in the form of positive feedback and a sense of personal achievement. You appreciate a simple thank you from a coach/manager, colleague or a customer. Regular praise is important and keeps you motivated. You may like this to be celebrated publicly or in a one-to-one setting. You may also be driven by extrinsic motivation in the form of status such as a promotion. Being recognised with large remuneration packages or material things such as cars, expensive clothes etc. will excite and motivate you.

PERSONAL DEVELOPMENT

You are motivated by a desire for continuous improvement. You will never be satisfied with your current skills and knowledge. You enjoy reading or going on courses. You will be more motivated by learning goals such as a Personal Development Plan (PDP) rather than strict performance goals such as business objectives and Key Performance Indicators (KPIs). You may choose a role due to the learning opportunity rather than the monetary reward. It is also likely that you are passionate about developing and mentoring others to help them achieve their goals. Attending courses, gaining qualifications and sharing knowledge is something you enjoy and value.

FREEDOM

You will want to have flexibility and autonomy when completing your tasks. It is important to you to be creative and allow things to emerge rather than be restricted by tight guidelines. Deadlines may not bother you as long as you can meet the deadline the way you want to. Although you may like some structure to how you do things, you will feel demotivated if you are pinned down with too many rules and regulations. You may appear a maverick due to your ideas and rebellious nature. You value your independence and expect to be trusted. Your motto may be "ask for forgiveness not permission". It is likely that you appreciate flexible working hours and being able to dress how you like.

FRAMEWORK

Structure, rules and systems are important you. You appreciate tidiness, order and stability. Clarity about the future is important and a well-planned approach will help you stay motivated. Therefore you may be risk averse if you don't have insight into all the possible outcomes. Constant change and unclear boundaries will demotivate you. Creating and implementing new processes will excite you. Without organised frameworks you may feel anxious and stressed and as a result you may become demotivated due to the lack of boundaries.

What is driving you to succeed?

All of the above are important and should be incorporated into your life to improve balance and happiness. Ignoring a sense of well-being can seriously affect your health and lifestyle. Being healthy and in control of your life will also translate into high performance. Those that can manage the balance between work/life balance and tenacity are likely to achieve sustainable results rather than short-term goals. Finding the right amount of freedom in the framework is key for success. Being rewarded for good work is essential to our biological make-up. It is also important to build in time to develop yourself for continuous improvement. Selfless acts of generosity will provide an intrinsic motivation and are a key component for successful leadership and high-performance teams.

On my workshops I encourage participants to number them one to seven, with number one being their main motivator. The top two to three will be more prominent than others and should be exploited. You may also find that they change over the years as your life and priorities change. When working with your team you can conduct the same exercise. They will learn about what motivates them and provide you with insight into how to get the best out of them. Motivation isn't that difficult to understand, yet it can be the most frustrating part of a manager's or coach's job. It involves being curious about your people and then designing an approach which works for each individual. You don't even need to guess, just ask them. Whenever I start working with someone for the first time, I always ask one question: "What role can I play to help you get the very best out of yourself?" It will take time, but it will be worth it.

It is important to know what motivates you and make sure you influence it in your life. The responsibility sits with you. Take action and do it now.

Looking back

When you look back at your life, when have you been most motivated? What has changed over the years? My motivations have changed during the course of my lifetime. At the age of nine I played most sports – tennis, cricket, football and rugby, the typical sports most young children play when living in England. I spent most days in my neighbour's garden kicking a ball around, taking turns at who plays in goal, who bowls, who bats etc. One day I noticed a pair of roller skates that belonged to his sister and without thinking or asking I put them on. Yes, they were a bit girly but I absolutely loved it. It felt different, a buzz that I had never felt playing other sports. My dad, who was more the traditional type, wanted me to play football so there were tones of Billy Elliott going on there. Having come from North London, my dad was a Tottenham Hotspur fan and season ticket holder. One of my proudest moments was when my dad and granddad came to watch me play football at my primary school practice on a Saturday morning. I remember scoring a hat-trick and then the three of us headed up to White Hart Lane. I would regularly go to White Hart Lane with my dad and I was an avid Spurs fan (no choice in the matter) and was often seen wearing my Spurs kit. However, I have to say I don't recall really enjoying watching the games. At age eight all I wanted to do was play football, not watch it.

Despite my love of football, my desire for roller-skating took over but it didn't come naturally to me. I couldn't stand up on them and was frustrated by my friend's ability to cruise around effortlessly on his. A few days later when skating on the patio, I picked up an old field hockey stick that belonged to my sister. Hockey was in the family. I spent many a wet and cold afternoon watching my sister play hockey for the county and for England. I had a spell playing field hockey myself in my later teenage years. I even considered dropping everything else and focusing on field hockey. I even set a goal to play for

Great Britain in the Los Angeles Olympics but I don't think it was my destiny and I'm glad to say I took the right path.

From the moment I picked up the stick my life changed forever, it was like a lightning bolt went through me. It's a very vivid memory for me. Being on roller skates carrying that stick felt like the most normal thing I had ever done at age nine and still to this day it gives me goose bumps just thinking about it.

Weeks passed and my neighbour invited me to the local roller disco. I wasn't any better at skating at this point – in fact I was awful, it is fair to say that I had zero innate ability. If I could just take five strides it was a triumph. I just wanted to go fast, but my body couldn't keep up with what my mind was intending. I would go home black and blue. I broke my arm twice in eight weeks, three times in two years! But nothing would deter me from persisting. For months I would go to the roller disco by myself, my other friends stopped going. I had a terrible time with bullying but the pay-off with learning how to skate distracted me from the bullies and I started to form new friendships.

It became clear to me that some form of hockey on skates existed. The skate marshals at the roller disco would strut around in their hockey shirts proudly showing off their team colours. Unlike my new creation using a field hockey stick, they were using ice hockey equipment. From that moment, street hockey embedded itself in my life. Street hockey became an obsession. I would practise every day after school and all day at the weekends.

By the time I was 11 there were hundreds of like-minded kids playing in the local car parks, school playgrounds and if we could afford it, the local sports centre.

By the age of 12, street hockey had established itself with leagues, tournaments and television coverage of the British National Championships, which happened to be sponsored by the lager Tennents Super – I'm not sure what their angle was there!

At its peak there were over 100 clubs in London alone. We would huddle round the TV and watch our heroes such as Eddie 'The Axe Man' Edutie and Rodney Roberts 'The General'. I wanted to be older so that I could play against them. The local older players played street hockey every Friday night at the sports centre. I would turn up and see if I could get a game but to no avail: "Go away Smiley, you're too young and you're not good enough." 'Smiley' was a nickname I had picked up at primary school due to what appeared to be a happy disposition. I am still stuck with the nickname today, except now I am referred to as 'Coach Smilee'. I changed the spelling as someone in my town growing up was also called Smiley, and was known for his supply of narcotics – I didn't want to be associated with that!

As I look back I think the 'happy disposition' had more to do with being nervous. I was one of those kids that couldn't stop smiling when getting told off by teachers. I have to confess that on reflection I was probably quite irritating. I would still return every Friday and watch just in case they let me play. Despite the push back, it simply didn't bother me, it didn't affect my passion for playing. I would find any opportunity to watch a game. I would focus on their every move and model myself on them. I started to imagine myself playing with and against them and as the years passed I developed, and that is exactly what happened.

The sport developed between the years1985 to 1992 and I am so grateful that I was able to play through the 90s with a team called the Tunbridge Wells Street Cruisers. Tunbridge

Wells is the town I grew up in and during this period 90% of young people either played or knew someone that played street hockey. If you are from the US or Canada that may sound normal but not in middle class Royal Tunbridge Wells. The Street Cruisers became infamous in Tunbridge Wells; as well as playing all over the UK we were competing in tournaments across Europe. There was no sponsorship and funds were low. We travelled in the back of a transit van which had the dual role of transport and accommodation.

We would head down to Dover on a Friday night, make the crossing to Calais and then head to wherever the tournament was taking place – Dusseldorf, Amsterdam, Lugano. When we arrived at customs in Dover, they would have a quick look in the window and shout "How many in the back?" There was always one extra that didn't have a passport and kept quiet, submerged by hockey bags. They would respond trustingly "Have a great time, lads" and we continued on our road trip. We competed against other clubs from Germany, Holland, Switzerland and Denmark. There was never any chance of becoming rich playing street hockey, it was about fuelling our passion, being the best we could be and that was plenty for us.

It was purely driven by intrinsic motivation. I think you can get far more out of individuals by igniting their internal motivations. I wonder if professional athletes would be any less passionate if they got paid the minimum wage. Unlikely – in fact they may be more passionate. It has been proven that extrinsic motivation is far less effective in the long run when any form of creativity is required. In Daniel Pink's brilliant book *Drive* he provides extensive evidence proving this. Ultimately, people want purpose and autonomy.

Great teams are motivated towards a single organising thought; what motivates you and the team members will vary. As a leader or a coach you'll have a responsibility to unearth the individual needs. Another thing I want to add which I feel is especially important is that the Street Cruisers did not have a team manager or coach. Input came from all the players, the actual role of leadership was shared throughout the team. Successful leadership isn't about creating followers, as many of the thousands of management books would lead you to believe. Creating followership is for those who need their ego massaged. Leadership is about integration, not followership. It is about facilitating and cultivating a high-performance culture, utilising the strengths, motivations and passion of your team members.

What motivates you?

After a period, I lost my motivation to play hockey – something I thought would never happen to me. I had thought that all the time I would be alive I would be on skates playing hockey. However, literally overnight I lost my motivation for the sport for some time. When I look back now, it was clear to see why. The players I grew up playing with and had so many great times with had retired and I no longer had the strong relationships I had while playing. I had lost the desire to develop further in the sport, and unlike in the past I was getting little recognition for how I was playing.

My three main motivators – personal development, recognition and relationships – were not being applied or utilised. On the flip side, I am extremely motivated in my work. I love my career, I am learning lots of new things working with great people and developing a strong reputation for what I am doing, thus all my motivations are being used. What's even more interesting is that since taking on the coaching job for Team GB I am extremely motivated and engaged with the sport. I am working and developing a great group of athletes; I am also developing as a coach and feel like I am making a difference. I have become less bothered about recognition in recent years and therefore replaced recognition with making a difference. I'm not saying recognition isn't important, it just isn't in my top three any more.

Focus on what you are great at

The most motivated people I know are those who focus on things they are great at. It is important that you identify with your strengths and what really motivates you so you can be truly successful in life, sports and in business. As discussed earlier, the biggest barrier to self-awareness and high performance is ego.

Unfortunately, from a young age you probably learned to identify with your weaknesses. It's not your fault – your football coach told you what you needed to improve on rather than giving the recognition for what you were doing well. Your teacher probably made you aware of the areas that you needed to develop, and your parents got you extra tutoring in the subjects where you had lower grades, all with the best intention of developing the all-round student. If your parents, teachers and coaches focused on what you were great at and got you extra support to develop those strengths, then you were very lucky and very unusual. This has been embedded into our culture and continues into adulthood. Even as a parent of a teenage daughter myself, I find that I am focusing on trying to develop Izzie's maths so she can keep up with her peers, not that I am any good at maths myself. The fact is she is great at singing, drama and art and, more importantly, she enjoys those subjects. I have to remind myself not to worry and continue to build her confidence in the subjects that she enjoys and will excel in. When was the last time your manager sat down with you and put a personal development plan together and focused purely on developing what you're already good at?

The Gallup Organisation surveyed over a million employees from a range of organisations and found that the most important aspect for talented performers was their relationship with their manager. Gallup also found, as described in Marcus Buckingham's ground-breaking book *First Break all the Rules*, that great managers and business leaders don't have an angelic view that they can create perfect individuals. They focus on getting the best out of their employees by utilising their strengths. Therefore they avoid their employees focusing on becoming slightly better at things they are not so good at which, for the record, can usually be delegated to someone who is good at that particular task. The problem with focusing on weaknesses is that we become demotivated; anyone who is demotivated will not perform as well and, as a result, it is likely that they will do less of what they are actually great at.

It is important that you identify with your own strengths and what you are passionate about. I truly believe that my career has developed through focusing on what I really enjoy. If I'm not passionate about something, I'm not doing it. Now that may sound a bit spoiled and of course there are things we all have to do that we may not like to do. Writing this book has seriously taken me out of my comfort zone. It involves a tremendous amount of planning and preparation, something that doesn't necessarily come naturally to me.

You can draw on your strengths and what motivates you and then apply it to everything you do. You will need to identify with what you are truly passionate about and draw on your past experiences where you have applied that passion and motivation. Then you can apply that passion to the most mundane tasks. Think back to what you really enjoy doing, what was it about the task that you enjoyed so much? It could be at work, a hobby or sport. It may also encourage you to consider what is missing from your team in the way of strengths and how you recruit the right talent.

Summary

We are at the halfway mark of this book having read parts one and two. By now you should know the following:

- What a winning mind-set is
- What the three principles of a winning mind-set are
- What it takes to move from good to great
- What your leadership style is
- How to copy (good) behaviour and do it better
- What motivates and drives you towards success
- The importance of playing to your strengths

In the next two parts of the book we will examine how understanding brain functionality plays a key role in enhancing performance, you will learn what all great athletes and leaders do to stay in the zone and what it takes to create a strategy for sustainable results.

PART THREE

STAY IN THE ZONE

CHAPTER 5

YOUR BRAIN

Before we explore what the zone is in this part of the book, we will firstly explore the brain and its connection with behaviour. In the last fifteen years, research into neuroscience has helped us to to understand behaviour and its relationship with performance. The brain is vital to our existence. It controls our voluntary movements and it regulates involuntary activities such as breathing and heartbeat. Neuroscience has become extremely topical, particularly in the world of sports performance. Whilst I don't want to oversimplify the brain in this book (the brain is far too complex), I will aim to help you understand the brain a little more deeply so that you can recognise your own behaviour and the behaviour of others. Research from neuroscience and technology such as functional magnetic resonance imaging (fMRI), as shown below, is the fundamental tool of cognitive neuroscience and has revolutionised how we understand what's going on in the brain. These brain scans have identified how certain behavioural preferences relate directly to performance. The brain has an innate ability to protect you – sometimes when you least need it.

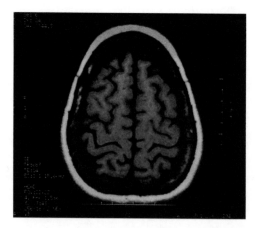

The British Cycling Team have benefited from the application of neuroscience, including athletes such as Sir Chris Hoy,

Bradley Wiggins and Victoria Pendleton. They had the good fortune of working with Dr Stephen Peters. In an interview with the *Daily Telegraph* after the 2012 Olympics, Peters said:

"When I work with people it doesn't matter too much what they are doing, I'm starting with what's inside their head and helping them understand that so that they can make choices and develop skills about using their emotions or holding back their emotions if they are interfering."

Your brain doesn't differentiate between stressful situations. Rory Mcilroy's brain doesn't differentiate between putting on the 18th hole for the Championship or being confronted by a grizzly bear. The brain simply recognises it as a threat, which can have a negative effect on your behaviour if not managed properly. It is likely that Mcilroy has developed the ability keep the championship-winning putt in perspective and through practice he has learned how to manage his emotions in this familiar situation. If he were to be confronted by a grizzly bear he may react very differently. At the same time there are people who are very comfortable amongst bears and have learned how live in their habitat. The point here is that self-regulation and emotional management is essential for competing at the highest level; this is what I refer to as 'Managing the Mist', the ability to focus and maintain clarity. It is what all the great leaders and athletes do. Furthermore, great leaders are able to create a 'mist free' environment to enable others to excel.

Different situations, jobs and levels of competition will require different levels of mental strength. You are biologically designed to run away from a threat or fight it. Without this instinctive behaviour the human population would have been wiped out a long time ago! Although the world has changed over the last billion years, you are still stuck with the 'Fight, Flight, Freeze' response. This response was useful 10,000 years ago when confronted by a sabre-toothed tiger. You had three choices: you would have attacked the tiger and taken it home for dinner; ran away and saved yourself; or frozen to the spot and become its dinner. However, this type of behaviour is not conducive to high performance in the workplace, competing at sports or in a social environment. Understanding how the brain functions will help you learn to compose yourself and make sense of the threat. Then you can refocus and turn a crisis into an opportunity. Staying in the zone will help you to manage your emotions in crisis, maintaining clarity of judgement and rational thinking, or what is known in neuroscience as taking the 'high road'. It is the ability to think rationally under pressure, and by doing so is a measure of your mental toughness.

Manage your fear

Let's put fear of failure into perspective by understanding the brain at a deeper level and why you are genetically built to respond to fear in a certain way. You will have done something in life that you have later learned to regret. This is normal, everyone has done it. It is likely that you have reacted to something instinctively without any real level of conscious thought and later reflected: What the hell was I thinking? Yes? Well, you weren't really thinking, the thought process was happening at 12 milliseconds (12 one-thousandths of a second) i.e. fast! This can also work in your favour when making fast decisions. These decisions are subconscious and very instinctive.

So why does this happen?

Several other essential parts of the brain lie deep inside the cerebral hemispheres in a network of structures called the limbic system. The limbic system links the brainstem with the higher reasoning elements of the cerebral cortex. It plays a key role in developing and carrying out instinctive behaviours and emotions and is also important in perceiving smells and linking them with memory emotion.

The limbic system is the part of your brain that reacts to the world around you reflexively and instantaneously in real time and without thought. For that reason it gives off a true response to information coming from the environment. The limbic system is also the emotional centre and it is from there that signals go out to various parts of your brain which in turn orchestrate your behaviours as they relate to emotions and your survival.

A key player in the limbic system is the amygdala, which takes its name from the Latin word for almond due to its shape. The amygdala is involved in processing strong emotions such as fear. It has been essential to your survival. You will instinctively respond to fear and protect yourself. Unfortunately, this amazing defence mechanism isn't always useful and can manifest itself as completely irrational behaviour, also known as taking the 'low road'. When this type of stress occurs you will feel a shift in your physiology, breathing will change and your posture will change. It is likely that you are unaware of these changes happening to you in real time and as a result it will also create the mist clouding your judgement. This stress can originate inside or outside your body. Examples of external stressors are loud bangs, a boss yelling at you, or looking up and seeing a piano falling towards you from the window of a tall storey building. Internal stress might be caused by feelings of depression or anxiety, perhaps through lack of purpose or an uncomfortable situation.

When you are under stress from a perceived threat, as shown in the diagram below, your hypothalamus sends a message to your pituitary gland, which activates the adrenal gland to secrete an increase in adrenaline in your body. This increases your heart rate and the contraction of skin blood vessels so that more blood goes to your muscles and brain. This will also cause you to fatigue much quicker due to the fact that you are using more oxygen and glucose. The response is likely to manifest itself as irrational behaviour. Have you ever got out of breath and sweaty in an interview when sat still in a chair? Hopefully this explains why.

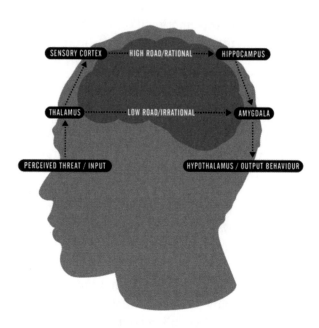

In order to achieve optimal performance you will need to manage the response to a threat and take the high road. The high road is much more thoughtful and methodical, albeit slower in its response. When an athlete is at his or her best, the low road and the high road are working simultaneously. The amygdala is preparing for any threat, working instinctively (non-conscious), whilst rational decision-making is also taking place at a conscious level. However, sometimes a deep-rooted fear will cause the amygdala to override any type of rational thought. A fear of spiders is a good example; with the exception of deadly poisonous spiders they are harmless. In the UK it is unlikely that you will encounter a dangerous spider, yet a spider running across the living room floor can cause hysteria in some people. It is likely that they are responding to someone else's fear of spiders and an image has been embedded in their unconscious that spiders are scary. It is completely irrational. I remember one time, not long before writing this book, a pigeon flew into the living room and I panicked, whilst my friend walked over calmly, put a blanket over the pigeon, carried it to the garden and let it free. I have a lasting memory since the age of five of a crow that had fallen down the chimney and was flying in our living room. The pigeon experience brought back an irrational fear of the situation.

Think back to all the times you have taken the low road and behaved irrationally. What caused it? If you had the chance to experience the situation again, what would you have done differently? Why does a highly paid English football player on £120k per week appear to struggle in a penalty shoot-out? The reason is the conscious mind, the 'inner critic' interferes and makes nasty little comments like: "You're going to miss, the goal looks tiny, the ball is heavy, the goalie looks huge." I wonder how many football players think: "What is the worst case scenario, so what if I do miss?" It is probably more like: "I don't want to be the player that is remembered for missing." Too late, that player has just written the script. Thoughts become a reality!

If you have had a similar experience in sport, the workplace or with relationships, it is your fear system detecting danger. The amygdala is very beneficial in dangerous situations; however, the key to high performance is the ability to override the response by making sense of the perceived dangerous stimuli. The amygdala does not even know what the threat is and overrides the mind's ability to rationalise the response. It is also one of the reasons why you may have a great experience and perform very well and then find yourself struggling. One minute everything is clear and the next your judgement is clouded by the 'white mist' causing you to feel intimidated, or you're getting the 'red mist' and becoming aggressive. I will share more details on the red and white mist in Part Three.

Irrational threats come in all shapes and sizes: for example, when playing sports you may fear making a mistake and letting your teammates down or it could be a person that causes you to act strangely when you're in their company. You will need to manage your fear and learn how to put the fear into perspective. Once you have isolated the fear and recognised it as an irrational response you can start to take action towards your goal. A coach can really help in these situations and I also think you can develop the awareness to work through it yourself. Developing your ability to 'manage the mist' will give you a huge competitive advantage over your peers in whatever role you are in.

Create new networks

I often hear of people that are going travelling to 'find themselves'. Apart from sitting in a dark room and fasting for a month, I'm not sure it is possible. The problem is your brain does not assemble thoughts and feelings from bits of information. It relates whole concepts to one another and looks for similarities, differences or relationships between them. The brain does not mechanically store the information that it acquires. It is changed forever each and every time it interacts with the world. So if you are thinking about heading off to Thailand or India to 'find yourself' you will actually be creating new networks, new images and experiences.

All the time you are trying to find yourself you will be creating a new self with new views, perceptions and opinions. It is nurture and nature working hand in hand that is creating your unique brain, which never loses its power to transform itself on the basis of new experiences that you have, and it can happen over very short periods. Your brain is different today than it was yesterday. A key discovery in neuroscience is the way in which you are able to 'grow your own brain' due to its elasticity. This scientific insight is an amazing opportunity for personal growth. It opens up possibilities and brings purpose to our life. Anyway, what are you supposed to do when you do find yourself? The whole point of life is to have purpose, set new goals and manage the gap between what you have and what you want.

The opportunity for you is to continue to develop, keep learning and pushing yourself outside of your comfort zone. Stretch yourself – what is the worst that can happen? During my sessions I use an elastic band as an analogy for stretching performance. An elastic band is only useful when it is being used or stretched. If you hold an elastic band in stretch for a long period of time and then relax it, it will become bigger than before it was stretched or in its comfort zone if you like. The more often you do this, the bigger the band will become. Conversely, if you overstretch the band it will snap. The brain is very much the same in this respect. The more you stretch yourself and learn new ways of doing things the stronger the connections in your brain become, what is known as a synapse connection and often referred to as neuroplasticity due to the plasticity of the brain. This is why I believe a coach or leader can be very effective. A coach can help you develop new positive ways of thinking therefore encouraging you to stretch and improve your performance as you work towards your goals.

Unfortunately, you may find that your inner critic, the conscious mind, tells you negative things that prevent you from stretching yourself or taking a risk. This may result in what is known as 'amygdala hijack', the irrational response to something that may not be a threat at all. This will cause inconsistency and frustration because you feel incapable of achieving what you set out to do. It is a barrier that you may feel powerless to overcome. It doesn't have to be this way at all.

Be consistent

The most successful athletes in the world are those that can deliver the same performance day in, day out, on every occasion. Many athletes I have spoken to put their ability to get in the zone down to their age or their experience. There is some science to this as the prefrontal cortex, which is responsible for voluntary movement and decision-making, continues to develop into the late twenties, therefore intelligence, motor control, cognition and attention continue to develop into the late twenties. This part of the brain is often referred to as the 'executive centre' due to its rational decision making capability, also known as the 'human brain' as it is the part of the brain which separates us from animals as pictured below.

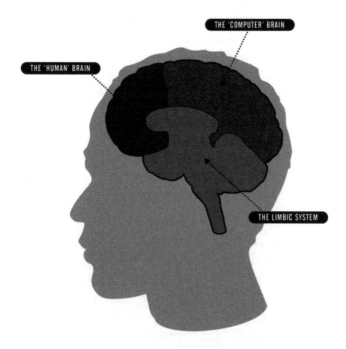

THE 'COMPUTER' BRAIN

THE 'HUMAN' BRAIN

THE LIMBIC SYSTEM

I believe this is why many sportsmen and women come of age in their late twenties and early thirties, provided they stay fit and healthy. The same can be applied in the workplace, particularly in leadership roles. You will develop and mature as a leader, experience will play a role, but the physical development of your brain will also help enhance your performance.

I didn't go to university to study organisational psychology until I was 36 – 20 years after I left school. I don't think I would have been ready any earlier, I'm not sure I would have been able to apply myself as well in my early twenties. I have interviewed hundreds of sportsmen and women during the last ten years who were in the autumn years of their career. I always asked them one question: "What would you do differently if you could do it all again?" As well as 'planning better' and 'appreciating the moment more', in many cases they responded by saying: "If only I knew then what I know now; I had speed and skill but I didn't have the composure and mind-set to take advantage of it."

I definitely wish I had had the knowledge I have now. When I was in my teens I would start preparing mentally for a tournament a month in advance on top of all the training I was doing. By the time I got to the competition all my attempts to be in the zone caused me to be mentally exhausted. I had generated too much adrenaline in my body when I didn't need it. I see players who try so hard preparing their mind for competition that it actually becomes a barrier to their performance. Some adrenalin is useful to gain some focus but too much, usually caused by anxiety and fear, will be counterproductive. I was always amazed at how certain athletes could just turn up to an event and appear so calm and relaxed. In fact it was very intimidating to see them so comfortable in that type of environment, chatting, smiling, like it was nothing more than a stroll in the park. Perhaps you have seen leaders speak effortlessly in front of large groups? When they walk into a room everyone notices. These people aren't getting in the zone, they are staying there! I made it my mission to understand this phenomenon; I wanted the formula for this inspiring talent.

Having the ability to stay calm in a crisis situation – for example, winning with seconds to go, making the game-winning jump shot, making a crucial leadership decision or delivering a crowd-pleasing speech – is a vital skill. Even when things are going well, focus on the game in hand. When things are going badly, stay calm and be aware there are always opportunities to get back in the game. Many of my clients are recruitment companies. Recruitment is a tough job and it can also be very rewarding. It is not uncommon to put a huge amount of work into a client, find them the perfect candidate, agree salary, terms and conditions and then for the deal to fall through. This can cause a Fight, Flight, Freeze situation. Those who panic and overexert their energy with the aim to fix the end result may cause more harm than good. Some recruiters withdraw entirely and do nothing at all. Top performing recruitment consultants are able to manage the mist, compose themselves, engage with the candidate and the client and fix the relationship. This type of behaviour is the difference between success and failure. As per Al Pacino's inspirational speech in the film *Any Given Sunday*, it is the inches that make a difference, the margin for error is all around us. Therefore you can have all the knowledge and skills in the world but if you can't develop the aptitude, tenacity and drive and simultaneously manage your emotions, all your talent will be wasted.

The Emotional Roller Coaster

When you are feeling under pressure, you may 'overexert' yourself and try to force a situation or you may 'withdraw' from the situation entirely. You may know people who get overconfident and they become overexcited; they are experiencing a rush of dopamine through their brain, the chemical associated with reward. As a consequence, they take more risks, they have become addicted to the feeling of success and what it brings. In which case they will forget about the process or system that helped them achieve success and only think about achieving more of the same. As they take more risks, mistakes start to happen. Then things start to slip, and they are likely to start to retreat or 'withdraw'. Their focus is on defending what they have achieved and their memory of the good times starts to fade, confidence is dropping. They have now stopped taking risks and have become stressed. They are officially on the 'emotional roller coaster'. As mentioned in Chapter Two, some will argue that it is this type of behaviour that caused the financial meltdown in 2008.

You will find yourself moving between different states, as you may become overconfident and you may overexert yourself in certain situations. You may also lack confidence and withdraw from certain situations. Many of these feelings are subconscious and feel beyond your control. The challenge is to stay present in the moment. Even the best athletes find this challenging. The conscious mind interferes all the time and affects performance. Your inner critic will challenge you daily. The good news is that you can develop a self-management system and increase your ability to manage the mist, as I will share with you in Chapters 6 and 7.

CHAPTER 6

THE ZONE

When you're in the 'zone' everything is clear, your vision is sharp, decision-making seems easier, your listening skills are enhanced and you have what all top athletes have: 'presence'. Some people simply have 'presence'. These are people who walk into a room and you know they are there before you see them, they seem to be able to speak with ease and fill a room with their voice, it resonates like a well-played tune and you want to hang on to every word. Great leaders, actors and athletes have it. They are completely at ease with themselves and they exude confidence. Roger Federer has it, Al Pacino has it, and President Obama has it. Were they born with it? Possibly. Can it be learned? Absolutely.

The zone is a place that every athlete wants to be in so they can compete at an optimum level. The zone has been described in a number of ways. In his seminal work *Flow: The Psychology of Optimal Experience*, Csíkszentmihályi proposes that people are happiest when they are in a state of *flow* – a state of concentration or complete absorption with the activity at hand and the situation. It is a state in which people are so involved in an activity that nothing else seems to matter (Csikszentmihalyi: 1990). Patsy Roddenburg in her wonderful book *Presence* refers to a similar place as 'Circle 2'. Second Circle presence is about being in the moment, and being in the moment keeps you open to change (Roddenburg: 2007). I have had the pleasure of meeting Patsy and attending her workshops, she is an incredible lady and I recommend her book. Much of her theory on Circle 2 energy has influenced both my own performance and my perception of what it truly means to be 'in the zone', particularly at a physical level. My goal has been to attempt to understand this concept at an academic and cognitive level through applying neuroscience.

When an athlete is in the zone, the subconscious takes over and he is playing on instinct, things appear to be moving slower and he is absolutely focused without the distraction of the conscious mind, allowing the conscious mind to focus on external tasks, limiting the amount of 'interference' from his inner critic as described in Part One. For example, the subconscious can allow an ice hockey player to skate and handle the puck whilst keeping his or her head up, managing to dodge checks from opposing players, whilst the conscious mind is 'thinking' and looking out for teammates to pass to. In some cases when you ask a player how they made an incredible game-winning pass, they can't answer your question, even the pass was subconscious. The ability to act instinctively and think consciously is a fundamental skill.

Driving a car is a good example; at first it is very awkward and done at a very conscious level. After practice it becomes an unconscious activity, allowing the mind to focus on observing the safety of the road, having a conversation with a passenger and changing radio stations. To truly develop a skill to an expert level it takes around 10,000 hours of practice; the more practice, the more likely you will have the resource to play instinctively and enable your conscious mind to focus on other things.

Sometimes I think people assume that top athletes and teams were put on the planet to annoy everyone else by consistently winning. They assume that they have some sort of innate natural talent. They don't take into consideration how much effort and practice has gone into becoming a champion. In Malcolm Gladwell's fantastic book *Outliers* he points to clear evidence that if you want to be at the very top of your game it only comes with practice. The more you take action, the more you will learn so get stuck in! A consistent performance was traditionally put down to 'muscle memory'. However, studies into neuroscience have discovered that there is no such thing as 'muscle memory', only 'mind memory' and it is the mind that develops and embeds new skills. It makes sense – how would you conceive there to be a memory in the muscle?

A motor skill is a learned combination of sequential movements that produce a smooth, efficient action in order to master a particular task. This development occurs in the region of the cerebral cortex that controls voluntary muscle groups. When a movement is repeated over time, the task can eventually be performed without conscious thought. It is every golfer's dream to master their swing; unfortunately, they may have developed bad habits and reversing this can be very challenging, albeit possible as in Nick Faldo's case. So if you are going to practise something, aim for a perfect practice. Through creating new habits you will reduce the attention required on the task at hand and create efficiency within the motor system in the prefrontal cortex of the brain. This in return will help you focus and improve your ability to stay in the zone.

The irony of the zone is that all the time you spend searching for it will become counterproductive for you. There is no zone to get into. This may come as a surprise to you as it is one of the Three Principles of a Winning Mindset. The aim isn't to 'get' in the zone, but to 'stay' in the zone. Every time you leave the house and drive to work you are in the zone. When you are socialising with friends or concentrating on an interesting piece of work you are in the zone. What you need to do is identify with what is throwing you out of the zone, which is usually a perceived threat resulting in lack of clarity, i.e. the mist.

The Red Mist

Let's explore what happens when you are not in the zone. I've had it, you've had it and you also know someone who has had it – the 'red mist'. It is fair to say that it takes longer for some people than others, but we all have our breaking point, we are biologically designed to do so. When you have been ejected from the zone, you are doing things without any rational thought. Your amygdala has been hijacked, you are on a speedway train along the low road. The receptors in your brain for noradrenaline have been influenced by adrenaline released in your body. Adrenaline is a hormone and is associated with increasing strength for short periods of time. This may be useful for physically lifting a car in a stressful situation to save someone's life. There have been a number of well-documented incidences of this type of superhuman strength.

However, in the workplace or in sport it will be less conducive. Whilst a little adrenalin can be useful to get you into action, the more excited you become, the more excited the amygdala will become. In this state, little thinking is taking place and all behaviour is instinctive. You're in 'fight' mode and you are overexerting yourself and forcing energy outwards. It is likely to result in a negative outcome. Your breathing has moved up into your chest and your posture is advancing forward. You are being perceived as aggressive by others. If someone sees you as a threat they will also respond in the same way and possibly 'lock horns' with you or they will retreat from you. You may have had a teacher, a boss or even a parent who reacted like this around you. How inspiring was it for you?

The White Mist

Although the brain is responding in the same way and taking the low road as with the red mist, this time you are feeling a sense of paralysis, you lack clarity and your vision seems murky. Your heart rate has increased and instead of travelling up into the chest, it has moved into your throat. Your posture has moved back on to your heels and your head has moved back, blocking the airway in your throat causing the pace of your breathing and speech to increase. Your energy is inward and you may find yourself withdrawing entirely from the perceived threat. As with the red mist above, your conscious mind is having little input into the shift in your physiology. Your inner critic has been turned up to full volume and is telling you to get out of what feels like an intimidating environment. Your self-esteem is at an all-time low. After the event you find yourself calming down, the mist clears and you are frustrated that you let it happen to you.

Have you ever wondered why you find yourself breathing fast when trying to speak? I remember the first time I asked a girl out, I felt like I had just sprinted a hundred metres and simply couldn't get my words out. My amygdala had taken over and the words I had practised simply didn't come out in the order I had rehearsed them in. This can happen in a business meeting, public speaking or a one-to-one with your boss, and it is very frustrating. The key is to prepare your breathing and rely on the words to articulate themselves from your subconscious, provided you have put the practice in. Breathing, as discussed later, is an essential factor when managing the mist.

Manage the Mist

The emotional response to a threat happens in a nanosecond. In this situation you could count to ten and wait for the mist to disappear, but in competitive sports or in the business world, ten seconds is the difference between winning and losing. The goal in a highly emotional situation is to focus your mind on managing your breathing and your posture. You can't control your emotions, it will only end in loss of control eventually. The aim is to be proactive. You will need to manage your emotions and prepare yourself for any potential threats that may come your way, like asking a girl out for instance! The analogy I use to separate control and management is likening it to driving a fast car. If you are driving fast and you approach a bend at speed and you 'control' the car by slamming on the brakes when you hit the bend, the car will spin out of control. The best approach is to apply the brakes early and accelerate comfortably round the bend. The latter is managing the situation by seeing what is coming and being proactive rather than trying to control a crisis.

Public speaking is an obvious example of a threat. I have learned to enjoy public speaking, although my first experience was a disaster. I had a severe case of the white mist, frozen to the spot, suffocated by the breathing in my throat, the pace of my voice was fast and I just wanted to get off the stage. I have developed a way to keep the fear in perspective. I ask myself what is the worst case scenario and find I can usually live with whatever I identify with. It helps me relax, my voice resonates better and then my speaking improves. Like anything we do in life, practice plays an integral role in improving performance, but you have got to get out there in the first place and practise. Experience equals performance improvement. Development isn't confined to just theory and classroom training. It only accounts for 10%, the real learning takes place in the action. This book will equip you with ideas, models and tools, but unless you practise them they will have little effect on your performance.

If you suffer with the red mist or white mist, it is likely that you have a 'trigger' or 'button' that gets pulled or pushed. It could be an irrational response to something that is connected to the past, yet subconsciously you make a link to it in the present. It could be the sound of a voice, the look of a person you meet or the environment you are in. In therapy terms this is referred to as 'transference'. A simple example is how you may instantly warm to a person or perhaps take a dislike to them. You are effectively transferring a subconscious image from the past on to someone new and reacting the same way in the present. The same could be said of an experience as child, perhaps speaking in class, being made fun of, etc. This may cause you to behave in a certain way, which could be entirely different from the person next to you, even though you are experiencing the same event. These types of reactions can be difficult to make sense of. This is a book on taking action from the present towards the future and is definitely not a book on therapy; however, we can all benefit with making sense of some deep-rooted experiences.

D.R.O.P. It

I usually avoid acronyms where possible and leave them to the gurus, although I think I may have finally found the real use for a stress ball! My clients have started using this process and it is successfully helping them to let go, explore new options and take action so they can move on in their life. The D.R.O.P. tool has been designed to help manage the mist, particularly the red mist.

As mentioned before, when we become stressed we release adrenaline and cortisol into the body. Whilst it is useful for short periods, it not healthy when we find ourselves stewing over something that has happened in the past, whether it is an old memory or a recent event. You will want to move on as quickly as possible so that you can focus on the next task. Spending too much time in one place is not healthy, and the simple fact is life is too short. You may find yourself lying in bed at night thinking about something and as you think about it you become more stressed, your heart beat increases, the thoughts are causing your body to create adrenaline and the chances of falling asleep in this state are very unlikely. As result, you start to suffer with sleep deprivation and a nasty cycle commences.

D.R.O.P. stands for Denial, Resist, Options and Proceed. It is a process and a self-management tool for taking ownership of the emotions that you may feel when you just can't let something go. The following describes what is taking place at each stage.

Denial

When you first start thinking about a situation that is causing you anger you are likely to start in a place of denial, you are taking no responsibility for your own actions. In this stage you are likely to be blaming others for the way you feel and you are angry with them. The more you think about their actions, the angrier you become. You are only interested in your own feelings when you are in denial. Talking to you in this state is pointless.

Resist

In this stage you are still looking outwards, you are resisting any idea of forgiving anyone for his or her actions. You are blinded by your own ego and the barriers are up. Letting go at this stage will make you feel vulnerable and this is the last thing you need. However, moving on is exactly what you need to do.

Options

With clarity and openness to what is taking place you will start to explore options, you may become more forgiving and empathetic. You will start to see things from another's point of view and will you start to put things into perspective. You are still looking outwards but instead of becoming defensive you are now being curious. You are asking questions to help you understand the situation better.

Proceed

Now with the mist settled, you have absolute clarity; you can see the route ahead and you are implementing the solutions that you identified in the Options stage. You feel calm and composed and ready to take the right action.

Next time you're reflecting on a stressful experience, grab a stress ball, squeeze hard, keep squeezing, squeeze it using the adrenaline you have created from whatever experience you have had. Continue to squeeze the ball while simultaneously and consciously slowing down your breathing – in through the nose and deep into the stomach, repeat it ten times. Talk yourself through the DROP process, and as you make your way through the options start to feel the tension in your body disappear. Move away from denial and resistance towards options and proceed; as you do, let go of the ball and feel the tension release. Repeat it several times if necessary.

Still today, occasionally my emotions get the better of me. I retired from international hockey in 2008 having discovered that I had degenerative arthritis in my right hip. Retiring is a pretty miserable time, I found that I had lost my purpose. Every workout in the gym, my diet and lifestyle had been focused around the World Championships. When I returned to the sport in 2010 to coach the British team, I naturally got the bug back and started playing again. Although I hadn't played for a while I had stayed fit; arthritic hips of this nature never get better so I thought I may as well keep playing until I got a new one! I was so excited to be back to playing competitive hockey again. I went back to my roots, playing in the South East of England league – not a great level but I thought it would be fun to play. During the first game I was welcomed back by a player who intentionally put the end of his stick into my mouth. It was actually the first time in my career spanning 28 years that someone had intentionally done that to me. I have a story for every scar on my face, equating to a total of about 50 stitches, although they have all been accidents. As you can imagine, I was furious but on this occasion I was able to compose myself, putting it down to the fact that he was a bit of a numpty.

The following week, a player clumsily decided to lift his stick over my head in an attempt to get past me, not quite clearing my head, and made a connection with my cheekbone, giving me a nice one-inch cut under my eye and a trip to the hospital. Not the best start for my return to hockey. Well, as you know these things tend to happen in threes. The following game was pretty intense, I was better prepared, and I had a mouthpiece to protect my teeth and a visor on my helmet to protect my face. However, during the game and unknown to me at the time, I had broken my rib. The problem with an injury like this during an intense game is that I couldn't feel it. I knew I had done something but it wasn't until the next day that I realised it was more serious.

As the game became even more intense, I could feel myself losing judgement and becoming angry about the way the opposition were playing. Although out of character for me, I was getting the red mist. As adrenaline rushed through my body disguising the feeling of pain, my brain's alarm system, i.e. the limbic system, had been set off, information was travelling via the thalamus to the amygdala and within milliseconds the amygdala hijacked my rational thought process and I was taking the low road. The hypothalamus, which is the brain's thermostat for keeping the mind and body at the right temperature, released cortisol into my body preparing me for the fight. The combination of cortisol and adrenaline focused my attention, but I was focused on the threat and not on what was required to win the game. As mentioned earlier, this was important when confronted by a sabre-toothed tiger when you have the choice of eat or be eaten, but it wasn't that situation at all. My life wasn't at risk, I just wanted to win, and my attention was in the wrong place. Due to the combination of cortisol and adrenaline rushing through my body during the game, I was using more glucose, which was causing me to fatigue quicker, thus losing clarity and judgement.

I became so angry about the way they were playing, becoming more aggressive and found myself in the 'sin bin' more often than I should have been for someone with my experience. The players on the other team could see how angry I was which encouraged them further. "Look at the Team GB coach," they laughed. "Whatever" I thought, knowing that they had got to me, but I had allowed the situation to get to me. I hadn't prepared myself for the game, I should have known I would be a target and should have prepared myself better. To use my analogy from earlier, I was driving a fast car and had slammed the brakes on when I was on the bend and had spun out of control. What annoyed me further was that it carried on for me after the game; I simply couldn't let it go. The more I thought about it, the more annoyed I became. Not only did it stay with me after the game, it continued into my 45-minute journey home. I noticed how I was driving fast and gripping the gear stick to the point that my forearm was starting to ache. I remember saying to myself: "Drop it Andrew, just drop it, practise what you preach!"

I started to breathe from the pit of my stomach rather than from my chest. I relaxed my posture rather than have my body pressed against the steering wheel. I wanted to let go of the gear stick, but I couldn't. Eventually my mind started to awaken and told me to loosen my grip and let go. I tried to apply the advice my brother always gives me: "If you can't let go, stop holding on instead." So I let go and the tension in my forearm disappeared and although I was still slightly angry, I started to feel better. It was this experience that inspired the D.R.O.P. tool.

I'd had a bad experience and I couldn't let go of the fact that some of the players were so ignorant and behaved in such a way that it was demonstrating a side of the game that wasn't appropriate, especially in front of young spectators. The anger was deep-rooted; their behaviour was impacting my values. I couldn't accept their behaviour and went into denial. I was also in denial about my own behaviour. I had fallen into a trap and was annoyed with myself for not being able to stay calm, which is something I have prided myself on and worked hard to battle with in the early years of my playing career. I had become known for my composure on the puck. Not only was I in denial, I was resisting the idea of forgiving them and accepting responsibility for my own behaviour, which was not conducive to high performance and I certainly wasn't role modelling the behaviour I would expect from my own players.

The one thing I did have in my favour during the game was that I was doing physical exercise. When your body generates cortisol and adrenaline your body biologically assumes it is going to run or fight, and therefore craves sugar and stores whatever it has. In my case I burnt the energy off so that it could not be stored as fat. This is not necessarily the case in the workplace, where there is no opportunity to do physical exercise. When continuous production of cortisol and adrenaline are combined with inadequate amounts of downtime for rest and repair, it will deplete your ability to respond appropriately and wears out your system. It is important that you build in time to stay fit and healthy, even if it is just a walk around the block at lunchtime.

The stress had made me irrational and my thought process didn't allow me to explore the options available. As I started to explore options the mist started to clear. I realised the players

I was competing against hadn't experienced what I had been exposed to in my career. They hadn't played in Anaheim, Vancouver and Las Vegas or represented their country 77 times. For them it was a game of hockey that they wanted to win. This was their reality; it was the championship game for them. I reacted to it inappropriately rather than taking advantage of it. It started to put things into perspective for me. Once I had explored the options I started to relax and was able to move on and proceed with a positive mind-set.

CHAPTER 7

UNLOCK YOUR AURA

Now that you understand both the cognitive and physical behaviours of staying in the zone, you will learn how to develop your 'presence'. As mentioned before, there are people that simply have presence. Presence gives off an aura of confidence but people often try to force aura. They exert their energy in a way that causes them to achieve the opposite of presence. We have already discussed over exertion and its link to the 'fight' response. People may feel threatened in an environment and put on a false bravado in order to protect themselves. They stick their chest out and invade people's space. They speak loudly to get attention. You know who I am talking about, we have all met one!

Presence is often associated with charisma, the sought-after leadership trait. I don't buy into this; I have met many leaders who may be perceived as having charisma but totally lack authenticity. Authenticity is at the cornerstone of achieving presence. Those with presence are simply comfortable in their own skin and have humility, they accept who they are. They believe they are 'good enough' although they don't believe they are too good. They don't feel threatened by certain company and are able to articulate themselves clearly in a one-to-one or large group setting. When they speak, their voice resonates, they maintain a steady breathing rhythm, their posture is neutral; they are neither withdrawn nor exerting energy. Even when they are in the company of someone who is exerting energy or has the red mist, they stay composed and relaxed. They hold their position and remain patient until the other person calms down and joins them. They are staying in the zone and not allowing anything to throw them out. They do not exert their energy to pull someone towards them who is withdrawn; they remain calm and patient so that the person feels more comfortable in their presence. It is impossible to communicate effectively with someone who has 'amygdala hijack'. The only way is to stay calm and be patient with them.

Warren Buffet is a great example of someone who is comfortable in his own skin; he is not tall in stature, he doesn't have the looks of a movie star. In 2008 he was ranked the richest person in the world but still remains humble. He doesn't own a Rolls Royce and is known for taking the subway rather than a chauffeur-driven car like many of his peers. Despite accumulating billions, he is still very much down to earth and maintains a high level of humility and authenticity. Another great leader of our time is Nelson Mandela; he exudes humility, he is one of those people whose presence you can feel before you know he is even there. Morgan Freeman manages to achieve a great portrayal of Mandela in the film *Invictus*. Freeman prepared for his role as Mandela by watching tapes of him to perfect his accent and rhythm of speaking. Although apparently he found imitating his presence very difficult, in an interview Freeman explained:

"I wanted to avoid acting like him; I needed to be him, and that was the biggest challenge. When you meet Mandela, you know you are in the presence of greatness, but it is something that just emanates from him. He moves people for the better, that is his calling in life. Some call it the 'Madiba Magic'. I'm not sure that magic can be explained."

I don't agree with Freeman's last point. I believe it can. I believe anyone can achieve presence, in fact I think Morgan Freeman's screen presence is an extremely good portrayal of Mandela. I have even shared scenes from the film on some of my leadership courses to illustrate presence. Great leaders, athletes, teachers and politicians have mastered this fundamental leadership skill. They have authenticity, gravitas and are perceived as extremely confident. Although internally they may actually feel nervous and shy, they are able to manage their thoughts, feelings and emotions and give off the impression that they are calm and in control. They appear tall, nonguarded and approachable. They will negotiate with you and they will lead you into a false sense of security with their calm and collected manner. They take time to listen – and not just the passive listening to show they are half interested, but deep listening. They pick up on your emotional state as well as what you are saying; in fact they are more likely to respond to your emotions than the words you are using. I've no doubt that you have met someone like this before. It is likely that their inner voice has a positive influence over them and not negativity. This is at the very core of being confident and unlocking aura.

Get Naked

For a moment, imagine that you have walked into a crowded room, it is busy, everyone is talking, you recognise some of the people and some of them are strangers to you. You feel awkward, people are talking but they aren't acknowledging you, you think they may be talking about you. Your body is paralysed by fear, every corner of the room seems like it is miles away. The feeling of anxiety is enhanced due to the fact that you are completely naked. Everyone can see that you are naked and there is nothing you can do about it. Then you wake up.

Dreams about being naked in a busy room can mean different things depending on the context. However, the one I have described is likely to have a meaning of feeling vulnerable or anxious; now imagine this:

You walk into a crowded room and you are wearing zero clothing. It doesn't faze you in any way, you approach people, and you meet them and greet them shaking their hand with a smile. You feel light, free and liberated. You have no concern with what people are thinking; they can think what they like about you, because you are comfortable in your own skin, you have an air of confidence about you, you feel tall, when you speak you feel calm and your voice resonates and fills the room. People listen and want to hear what you have to say. They haven't even noticed that you are naked.

This type of dream suggests that you are absolutely comfortable in your own skin. Have you ever noticed how someone can get away with wearing a scruffy tee shirt and still have a presence? Getting comfortable with being naked in a crowded room is a metaphor for unlocking your aura. You are effectively stripping off the layers or the 'armour' you are using to protect your ego. An egoless life is a free life. Getting comfortable with your vulnerability is the key to freeing yourself from fear and anxiety. Presence isn't achieved by the person who can shout the loudest, stick their chest out and get noticed; it is about being humble, open to change and letting go of your ego. Presence is not just great looks either. You can look great and still shrink in a room or on stage if you do not project yourself properly.

During the 'Manage the Mist' workshop we help participants develop presence and their ability to stay in the zone by focusing on breathing techniques and posture. One technique involves breathing in through your nose and deep in the pit of your stomach. You can try it now. Put your hand on the lower part of your stomach just above your waist; breathe in deep so that it pushes your hand out. Try doing it ten times slowly and notice how relaxed you become. Another exercise that I recommend, particularly if you have trouble sleeping, involves lying on your back either on the floor or in bed. Bring your feet up to your backside so that your knees are bent. Use the same breathing technique as above. To ensure that you are breathing low enough, put a coin over your bellybutton and focus on pushing the coin up as you take deep breaths in through your nose. If your chest comes up, it is an indication that you are not breathing low enough.

I also ask participants to stand with their hands by their side with a neutral stance. Many of them find it very hard not to put their hands in their pockets or cross their arms. It causes them to feel too open and awkward. Have you ever stood in a bar without a drink in your hand? It feels uncomfortable doesn't it?

Find your voice

Denzel Washington, who I think is a very cool and relaxed actor, said in an interview with the BBC that he always takes 40 slow breaths before every scene. I recommend this before delivering a presentation or any in type of situation that you may feel threatening; it will help you relax so that you will articulate yourself better. Roddenburg refers to this as 'talking on the breath'. This involves applying the same breathing techniques as above and only speaking when you breathe out, then controlling your breathing so that you can continue the rhythm. Apparently Margaret Thatcher was a master at this in interviews and the technique would prevent interviewers from interrupting her. She was one of the great orators and speakers of her time, known for her conviction and clarity, and despite having many enemies she still managed to win three consecutive elections. The ability to resonate and be heard can seriously affect your leadership career and the ability to influence others. Sounds obvious but if you don't manage the mist, the pace of your voice will increase and you will no longer have an impact on those you are communicating to, people will instinctively pick this up. For example, when I get the red mist with my teenage daughter (what parent hasn't?), she looks at me as if I am a lunatic and I immediately lose credibility with her, plus it causes her mist to rise and we get nowhere. However, when I slow my voice down, talk on the breath, maintain eye contact, it has much more impact and she knows I am serious.

It is the same when delivering a keynote, a boardroom presentation or giving someone feedback. If you want to influence people, improve your negotiation skills, or deliver a key message, it starts with your ability to compose yourself. Anyone in a leadership position who cannot manage the mist and stay present in the moment is doing themselves and their team a serious injustice.

On our workshops and coaching programmes we also help participants with their image as part of developing their personal strategy. Whilst external perception may not seem important to some people, they will still project an image to the world, which is important for their personal branding. Barack Obama is another great example of someone who has presence and extremely good branding. His ability to connect with the audience during his run for presidency was beyond anything I have ever witnessed. It doesn't matter whether you are introverted or extroverted, white, black, short, tall, thin, fat, beautiful or any less attractive than the next person. Anyone can develop presence. Dustin Hoffman has huge presence, but let's face it, he's not that great looking, he certainly isn't tall, but due to how relaxed and comfortable he is in his own skin he creates an undeniable screen presence that resonates with his audience.

Next time you walk into a busy bar or a conference, I challenge you to walk into the middle of the room, look around the room, breathe out and remember that you are 'good enough'. Take notice of what happens to your breathing and your posture. Do you find yourself wanting to get out of there, withdrawing from the situation, or are you puffing your chest out, exerting energy and bracing yourself? Try to stay neutral, calm and manage the emotions you are feeling, keeping the breathing in through the nose, low into the belly and breathe out to the room. When you speak, take your time, breathe in and speak as you breathe out, talking on the breath. By doing so you will save energy, you'll reduce the amount of glucose and oxygen being used by the brain. Watch how the white mist settles and how sharp your vision becomes. You will be surprised how people not only see your aura but also feel it. You have presence and you are present, taking in everything around you, all five senses working simultaneously, you're in the zone and feeling strong and bold. Enjoy this moment – when you do this successfully you will create an aura around you and people will want to know who you are. Like anything in life, unlocking aura takes practice and it is a conscious choice you can learn to make. As the mind becomes more comfortable and you make new neural pathways in your prefrontal cortex, you will soon create new habits and behaviours that will embed themselves into your subconscious. Remember the brain is elastic, you are continuously growing and developing and this will continue throughout your life.

CHAPTER 8

EMBRACE FAILURE

*"I've failed over and over and over again in
my life and that is why I succeed."*
Michael Jordan

In this chapter we will explore failure and success. I will share
my personal journey from playing in the car parks and sports
centres of Tunbridge Wells to representing California in Las
Vegas. I will share how I overcame my own limiting beliefs
and learned to manage the mist. Malcolm Gladwell, author of
Outliers would refer to me as an outlier. An outlier is a scientific
term to describe things or phenomena that lie outside normal
experience. Now this may sound like I'm blowing my own
trumpet here, which is not my intention – in fact quite the
opposite, let me explain what I mean. I played at the highest
level possible at inline hockey between 2000 and 2004 and
until 2012 I was the only British player to do so, but it doesn't
necessarily mean that I was the best. I'm no prodigy, I certainly
wasn't a natural when I first started playing, as I described
earlier.

What actually took place was a series of events that positioned
me perfectly to take advantage of what was in front of me. For
example, Tunbridge Wells was a hotbed for skating and it had
one of the biggest roller discos in the country. As a consequence,
street hockey emerged and the players I eventually played
with were older and six years more experienced than me,
so my benchmark was way beyond most people in my age
category. Living close to Dover meant we could access Europe
more easily than other teams in the country, resulting in more
travel and exposure to a better standard of hockey. I was also
fortunate to have Jock in my life – he taught me how to be
more professional. I had parents who could afford to buy me
hockey equipment and a great mum who drove me around the
country to play.

There are a number of things that have presented themselves to me that have helped with my success. So was I lucky? If so, alternatively you could look back on my life and say I was unlucky. My dad sold the family business when I was 11, he then went on to lose all his money in the construction industry in the late 1980s, I grew up in what would be described as a dysfunctional family and my dad passed away when I was 16. It is all down to perspective.

I would argue that there is no such thing as luck and it is more a case of effort, openness to change and embracing the unknown. Gladwell provides extensive evidence that suggests the time we are born, the environment that we grow up in and the people we meet can dramatically influence our success. He provides examples such as the Beatles, Steve Jobs, Bill Gates and many more, explaining what series of events caused their success. This doesn't mean success is outside of an individual's control but if we don't take advantage of the opportunities that are often presented to us we may never reach our full potential. We are constantly surrounded by opportunity and it is those who are prepared to take a risk, embrace failure and therefore make the most of the opportunity that achieve success. This once again requires the ability to manage the mist and maintain clarity in order to make effective decisions.

What is this word failure?

"Life is ten percent what happens to you and ninety percent how you respond to it."

It appears to me that the word failure means different things to different people. Are those with a winning mind-set people who simply do not fear failure? I don't think so, everyone will be threatened by something; as discussed earlier, we are biologically designed to do so. It is how they channel their fear of failure that counts. Lou Holtz, one of the premier College American Football coaches of all time said: "Life is ten percent what happens to you and ninety percent how you respond to it." I believe this is so true, and the science proves it.

I have spoken to top performers who say they are driven to succeed because of the fear of failure. The idea of actually failing is enough for them to do whatever it takes to succeed. However, these people also tend to become stressed as they attempt to avoid failure and push it away. This can cause them to 'slam on the brakes' to stay in control only to encounter the red mist, therefore becoming counterproductive. I have also observed and interviewed people who will not take on a challenge if they believe that the goal is unachievable. They appear to avoid any possibility of failure by not even taking on the challenge in the first place. They say: "Well if I can't win what is the point?" The point is how will you learn if you don't take a risk? Any type of decision-making is going to involve some degree of risk.

There are also many people out there who simply don't believe in themselves, they suffer from limiting beliefs and withdraw from situations, usually suffering with the white mist rather than just going for it to see what happens. They could embrace the learning experience rather than focusing on the end result. Deep down we all want to win, it is in our nature, whether you believe it or not. If you had the choice of taking first or second place, you would take first place. Even if you're one of those people who feels guilty when beating the other person, it still feels good to win. To be truly successful and achieve a 'winning mind-set' you will have to accept failure is a possibility and find a way to let go of any fear that you have of failure. The point is whenever there is a learning opportunity it is a form of winning because you are gaining even more experience. The other important point is that when we embrace failure we relax more, achieve clarity and take advantage of the opportunities in front of us. Whatever camp you fall into, the first step in embracing failure is to accept that failure is a possibility and then ask yourself what is the worst case scenario? How do I feel about it and what action can I take to avoid it happening? The following four steps will help you do this and achieve more than you ever expected.

Embrace Failure and Take Action

The Four Steps:

1. Accept failure is a possibility.
2. What is the worst case scenario?
3. Put it into perspective.
4. Take action!

Step 1 – Accept failure

You will make mistakes, things will go wrong, and nothing will ever be perfect for you no matter how much you plan or practise. The only way to really enhance your performance is to get out there and have a go. Having experience is the only way to learn; with experience you will have something tangible to reflect on, to review and conceptualise so that you can move on and try again and do it even better. If you avoid accepting that failure is a possibility, it will cause you to over exert energy, becoming forceful and controlling (red mist). Or exhibit withdrawn energy and a feeling of paralysis (white mist).

Step 2 – What is the worst case scenario?

Now that you have accepted that failure is a possibility, the next step is to consider what the worst case scenario is. It has to be the very worst before you can move to steps three and four. You will have to identify with the lowest point. I have worked with a lot of sales people who fear making business development calls. They become threatened by what the potential customer might say. This causes activity to drop. When they do make the call they may sound nervous and no one is going buy from someone who sounds timid and nervous.

Step 3 – Put it into perspective

The third step is to put the worst case scenario into perspective. Ask yourself what is really at stake here. Although the idea of accepting that you may not achieve your goal is a depressing thought for you, when you compare it to things in your life and what others are going through, is it really all that bad? Once you can put it into perspective, notice how the stress leaves your body, how your breathing slows and moves to the pit of your stomach rather than your chest or throat. You will gain clarity and focus and as a result your performance will improve. As with the sales person making prospect calls, they became more relaxed, they resonated better on the phone and sounded more assuring to the client.

Step 4 – Take action

The fourth step is the most important. Without action the first three steps will be a waste of time. Now that you have clarity, you are feeling relaxed and focused, you will need to take action towards your goal. You have lost direction and found yourself in a rut. It takes effort to get out of a rut but you can't force it. The excitement of moving forward will generate a little adrenalin – stay in the zone and, most important of all, take action!

Overcoming limiting beliefs

I often suffered with the fear of failure and was a victim of the white mist around the time I started to play at a more competitive level. In August 1996 Tunbridge Wells Street Cruisers travelled to Chicago to play in the North American Roller Hockey Championships (NARCh). It was a chance to test us against the best competition in the world. NARCh was and still is today the most competitive club inline hockey tournament worldwide. Having played in America with the London All Stars the previous two years, I thought we would be able to compete with some of the best teams. But NARCh was different; it was the pinnacle of our sport. There were three divisions – Silver, Gold and Platinum – and we played in the Gold division (Division 2) and were seriously out of our league!

It was much tougher than we expected; we played three games, lost 11-3, 5-2 and 8-0 (twice victims of the eight goal mercy rule, where the game ends when there is an eight goal difference) and were very quickly disposed of. It is embarrassing to ask the opposing team not to score at 7-0, having to explain that we had travelled 5,000 miles and would like to play the entire game, then for the game to end seconds later. It is a further embarrassment to celebrate a 5-2 loss, simply because we played the game to the end. I remember watching the NARCh Platinum final, sitting in the arena in awe of the incredible professional athletes before me, admiring their speed, power and skill on the rink. I actually felt quite demotivated that my abilities were so far away from that of those players. My goal of being a pro no longer seemed achievable. By self-diagnosis I was suffering from 'Limiting Belief Syndrome'.

On my return to England I was inspired by the hockey I had seen, but I found it difficult to adjust to the idea that my goal appeared to be unrealistic. I had to accept that it may not happen, and by accepting it I noticed a shift in my 'mind-set'. It wasn't a quick process; it took time to accept how my ability compared before I could explore new options. Once I had finally accepted it, I no longer felt demotivated. I started to focus my attention on playing and being the best I could be – nothing more, nothing less, just the best I could be, living in the moment. I was going to push myself to the limit and that was my new goal. I read every book about coaching, I started to coach more myself, watched every DVD on the market, I subscribed to American magazines, I read about players. I studied the type of training they were doing in the gym and how they developed their skills. I followed the progress of a particular player, a Canadian by the name of Victor Gervais. He was the top goal-scorer for Anaheim in the professional hockey league and a member of Team Canada. What was he doing? How could I be as good as him? How could I model his behaviour?

Embrace the unknown

It was also clear to me that if I was to improve my performance and play at the highest level, I would have to move and play at that level more consistently. So as part of my strategy, in August 1997 I scraped some cash together, packed my hockey gear and booked an open ticket to Vancouver. It was a huge risk; I had very little money and nowhere planned to stay. I had made some enquiries to the local leagues in Vancouver prior to travelling out. I had a contact named Dave Collier, his family owned a roller hockey rink in Langley, a small town just outside Vancouver. It had several leagues, my plan was to find a team to play for and then hope for the best.

After 36 hours of travel and a few problems on the way via New York (which is a story in itself!), I finally made it to Vancouver. I had budgeted for a week's stay in a hotel, which

I hadn't booked. Typically, the 1997 Indy Car Race was taking place in Vancouver, so everywhere was booked up.

I had no option other than to call Dave. He was the only person I vaguely knew in the entire country. The conversation went a bit like this.

"Hi Dave, it's Andrew."

"Who?"

"Andrew, from England."

"Oh, hey Andrew, how are you? Still thinking about coming over?"

"Erm, yes, actually I am here, unfortunately there is nowhere to stay, because of the Indy Race in Vancouver."

"Oh, OK, well why don't you come to Langley, and we'll see if we can find you a hotel here?"

"Great, how do I get there?"

"You need to get the Sky Train from Vancouver to Surrey, in Surrey you need to get a bus to Langley, you get off at 64th and 200th. Look for Mufford Crescent, there is a Canadian Tire store (bit like Homebase) on the corner, walk down Mufford Cresent and you'll see the rink on the right."

Now bear in mind it had been 48 hours since I had left home and I had been walking around Vancouver downtown all day with hockey equipment and luggage. It was 10 o'clock at night, I was feeling fatigued and was thinking to myself: What the hell is a Sky Train? And what does 64th and 200th mean, and what is a Canadian Tire?

Eventually I made it to Langley, which seemed like hours. I found Mufford Crescent and proceeded down a dark road, like a country lane, emphasised by the cows in the field adjacent. Then in that moment, the realisation kicked in. I'm in Canada, but where? I'm walking down a dark road; there can't be a rink down here, can there, what have I done, how did I get here? And then, like a vision, there it was in big lights – West Coast

Roller Hockey Arena. At the time, I didn't fall to my knees with my hands in the air with light shining on my face, but my memory now is exactly that!

I arrived at the rink at 11.00 pm; I was sweating and slightly delirious. Scott, the rink manager greeted me immediately: "You must be the English guy." Five minutes later Dave walked in, it turned out he had been driving around trying to find me. Unfortunately, all hotels were booked out in Langley too. Fortunately, Dave had arranged for me to stay with his parents that night, until I could find something. It was extremely generous of them, considering they had never met me. I always thought Canadian people were generally warm and welcoming people; as it turned out, Dave's parents were from Bolton, England.

Scott asked if I'd like to skate at midnight as there was a team practising, preparing for NARCh which was taking place in Vancouver that year. Of course I couldn't say no, I had a quick 45-minute nap and played that night. Two days later I found myself playing in the Vancouver Breakout Tournament. The Breakout Tournaments ran across North America and were played outdoors in car parks or 'parking lots' to use the local terminology. This was the perfect start for me; I had grown up playing outdoors and was more than comfortable on asphalt. It was 90 degrees, our team was named Hawaiian Punch, initially to be a bit of fun, we even wore Hawaiian beach shirts to play in. I played well and scored plenty of goals, our team won the Vancouver Breakout and as a result we each received a new pair of Nike skates. I had firmly positioned myself as a player in Vancouver and things were looking positive.

After a week playing back at the rink, however, I quickly became aware the level was much higher than back home. I went from being one of the top players in the UK to a less than average player in Canada. My first game was for a team in the

5th division. The game was very different in North America and I found it very hard to adapt. In the UK we played with a ball and in Canada it was with a puck, the rink was four times the size of the local sports centre that I was used to. I also managed to guest for the Dusseldorf Rams in NARCh along with two players from the Street Cruisers who travelled over for the tournament.

A few weeks after the tournament my friends made their way back to the UK, I got a job at the rink working on the concession serving up drinks and pizza pops and I also cleaned the rink floor every night. It covered my rent and allowed me to practise every day. I also joined a gym to help with my strength. During the following five months, I gained 20 pounds in the gym and I was at the peak of fitness. I was skating faster and shooting harder.

The hard work paid off. I was eventually selected to play for a team called the Vipers, along with fellow rookie Kirk French. The Vipers competed in the 1st division, I was so excited and pleased to be playing at that level. I felt strong and confident;

my game was ten times better than when I first arrived in Vancouver. Everything was perfect, at least up until the first game. Despite having improved my skills, I couldn't adapt psychologically. I compared myself to the players around me; several players had represented Canada and played in the professional league. I felt inadequate and paralysed by the fear of failure. I was taking the low road and I had a severe case of 'amygdala hijack'.

After the game it all seemed so irrational. I knew I could play at that level; I had the skills, in fact I had more skills than a couple of the players on the team. I thought back to my vision and goals: I'd achieved everything I had wanted to so far but something was missing. I would share my frustration with Kirk, who had no problem adjusting and was very comfortable on the rink. The coach told me that I had the skills and I needed to learn how to play the game better, but this was psychological. I had an inner voice booming in my head that I wasn't good enough and it was a potential barrier to achieving my goals. It was like I couldn't see anything on the rink. This wasn't just white mist, it was thick fog! I was making ridiculous mistakes that I would never usually make. It felt like everyone was watching me and judging my performance.

Something needed to change. I started to go through a process, asking myself the same question I'd asked myself when I returned from Chicago. I also remembered what I had learned a few years earlier from the Carnegie books. What is the worst case scenario here? So what if I don't play well, then what? I guess I'll head home, then what and then what? Once I identified with the worst case scenario and put it into perspective, I was able to accept it as a possibility and let go of the fear of failure. It was challenging for me, especially for someone who wants to win on every occasion; to accept failure seemed counterintuitive. Not competing at the highest level was a depressing thought. But once I compared it to things in my life and what others were going through, my life seemed pretty good, it really didn't seem all that bad. As a result I became relaxed, the fear drifted away and the mist disappeared. I gained clarity and took action towards my goal. This transferred itself on to the rink and I started to perform better.

My conscious mind had rationalised my fear of failure. The perceived threat in the form of failure was causing me to take the low road and as a consequence I withdrew from the situation, I didn't want to be there. It was my natural primitive response to fear kicking in. As we have already discussed, this is not useful in sport, business or socially.

Your ability to make sense and rationalise your fear or perceived threat that you are encountering is the difference between winning and losing. There is a difference between expecting failure and accepting that failure is a possibility. Remember, our expectations and our thoughts become a reality. If you expect to fail it is an invitation for that to happen to you. If you can accept that things may go wrong, you will relax. In a relaxed state or in the 'zone' your performance will improve. This forces you to become more self-aware, accept your ability and not allow your ego to get in the way of your development. Once this has been identified you can work on reaching your full potential. Self-awareness and developing mental toughness is key to success. It is the ability to identify with your strengths, behaviours and weaknesses and manage any limiting beliefs you may have.

I dealt with my fear of failure; I saw the season through to the end with the Vipers. On my return to the UK I signed a contract with Nike where they supplied me with equipment and enough clothing and shoes to open a Nike store. The following year I played for the California Slipjacks in Las Vegas. I was top goal-scorer and we won the Gold medal in the Platinum

Division, something I once thought was impossible. In 2004 the Slipjacks were promoted to the Professional Division. Unfortunately, we didn't win but my greatest memory was at the beginning of a game at the face off. I looked up at the player opposite me on their team. Standing in front of me was Victor Gervais; he may have been a veteran then, but he still had it. In fact his team won the Pro Division that year. I couldn't believe it, like the vision and thoughts I had of playing against Gervais had just become a reality. I was 28 at the time and I behaved like a 16-year-old girl at a Beatles concert! Well, not that bad but it was a very cool moment.

My trip to Vancouver was a risk; it could have gone in an entirely different direction for me. It was worth the risk, it paid off for me – sometimes you just have to go for it. Was I lucky that I met Dave Collier and his parents? Was I lucky that I was able to play every day because the family I lived with owned the rink? Did I get lucky when asked to play for the Vipers? Was the Nike sponsorship deal lucky? What I do know is that unless I had embraced the unknown, been open to change and conquered my fear of failure, none of the above would have happened.

Today I apply my fear management system to most circumstances. I have also helped hundreds of people come to terms with failure and how they manage a perceived threat. As I mentioned before, there really isn't a zone to get into. You are already there; the challenge is staying there. It is your perception of a threat that will throw you out and create 'the mist'. All you need to do is change your perception of the threat and you'll find yourself in a relaxed state. In a relaxed state you will perform and behave better.

My experience and the experience of others have proved to me that nothing is impossible. Our thoughts become a reality. If you want it, it is there for the taking. We need purpose, self-awareness and the ability to embrace failure. Nothing is impossible if a common goal is in place, whether it is world peace, an end to poverty or England winning the World Cup. Visualise your goals, see yourself acting them out, be brave, stay focused and follow your dream – and dream a lot. Be prepared for the opportunities that present themselves to you, take a risk and hold on to what you're truly passionate about. After all, what is the worst that can happen?

I have made more mistakes than I can remember – some so bad it cost my team the championship, more than once! I have no doubt that I will make more mistakes in the future and so will you. However, a successful life isn't a life without failure. Success is measured on how you recover from it.

You may know this poem by Walter D. Wintle called *The Man Who Thinks He Can*. I think it hits home some of the key messages so far in this book.

> If you think you are beaten, you are;
> If you think you dare not, you don't.
> If you'd like to win, but think you can't
> It's almost a cinch you won't.
> If you think you'll lose, you've lost,
> For out in the world we find
> Success being with a fellow's will;
> It's all in the state of mind.
>
> If you think you're outclassed, you are:
> You've got to think high to rise.
> You've got to be sure of yourself before
> You can ever win a prize.
> Life's battles don't always go
> To the stronger or faster man,
> But sooner or later the man who wins
> Is the one who thinks he can.

"Failing at something is acceptable, accepting you're a failure is not."

PART FOUR

HAVE A STRATEGY

CHAPTER 9

WHAT IS STRATEGY?

So far in the previous chapters we have focused on enhancing personal performance. We have worked through two of the three principles: 'self-awareness' and 'stay in the zone'. This part of the book will help enhance your leadership skills, develop your team strategy and create winning mind-sets. The methodology I am going to share with you is focused on developing a high-performance team based on my own experiences coaching at an international level, and conversations with professional athletes and business leaders. Whether you are a business owner, team manager or coaching a sports team, you will find this next section very useful.

Strategy

The word strategy appears to have mass appeal in the workplace. Life can seem pretty dull around the table until the conversation shifts to business strategy. A workplan is just a workplan until it becomes a 'strategic workplan'. Business planning gets exciting when it becomes 'strategic business planning; aligning the organisation makes sense but only gets interesting when 'strategic alignment' is considered.

Today, strategy is more concerned with business, although it has its origins in the military. In fact the word strategy comes from the Greek word meaning general. There are a number of variations of strategy and at different levels. The three main levels are corporate, business unit and operational. This book is mainly concerned with operational and team strategy. The concepts can be applied to any team in both business and sports, and across cultures. However, I would argue that the concept could also be applied at a corporate or organisational level.

Corporate strategy is concerned with the overall purpose of the business to meet stakeholder expectations. Business unit strategy is concerned more with how a business competes successfully in a particular market and operational strategy is concerned with how each part of the business is organised to deliver the corporate and business unit level strategic direction. A successful corporate strategy is defined by how well alignment is achieved throughout the organisation. Every team should have a common purpose, whether it is a sports team or a business team. It will need to be aligned to the organisation's vision. Not only should it be aligned to the vision but also to organisational objectives, processes, values and branding. Whilst a vision is not a strategy, it must start there.

Emergent versus planned

The two main types of strategy are planned or emergent strategy. Planned strategy is based on analysis, logic and rational thinking. I have to say I'm not convinced that in such a fast and volatile environment you can possibly execute a planned strategy – certainly not one that is linear. A plan can be too formulaic and linear and unlikely to be successful in today's changing environment. The only thing we can really plan for is change itself. Often the type of strategy is chosen due to the preference of the person devising the strategy, which eventually determines the company culture. I have learned this playing team sports. When a coach has a preference for systems it is great for creating understanding and a consistent approach. It can also stifle creativity and the ability to adapt to change. At the same time, a lack of systems can cause chaos and uncertainty. Ultimately, behaviour drives everything and we know that behaviour is created in the brain. We know that brains have elasticity; they are malleable, organic and forever developing and therefore so are teams and organisations. Things will change; the only way to cope with change is to be proactive and adaptable.

Create a framework for success

I recommend that you create a 'framework' rather than a plan. Creating a framework where flexibility, freedom and autonomy can be achieved is more likely to result in success. For me a framework falls between planned and emergent. By doing so you will achieve 'freedom within the framework'. I introduced this concept to Team GB Inline Hockey in 2006 when I had the role of player/coach. I felt the players needed direction on how to play the game in the way of systems, but I also wanted them to show their creativity when necessary. This enabled us to flex and adapt depending on what the opposition had for us. It is up to you how tight you think the framework needs to be. The speed of development in technology is driving the pace of change so it is extremely difficult to predict what is going to happen next. The aim is to anticipate the next move as best you can. As arguably the greatest ice hockey player of all time, Wayne Gretzky, once said:

"A good hockey player plays where the puck is. A great hockey player plays where the puck is going to be." The same must be said in business and in all walks of life. Your strategy will provide you and your team with direction and insight into how you achieve your vision. The aim of a good strategy is that it will help you stay focused especially when you doubt yourself and your 'inner critic' tries to throw you off track. A well thought-out strategy will provide you and your team with direction and purpose. Let me illustrate my point about the story of the Hungarian platoon described by Karl Wick. Miroslav Holub bases his account on a poem about a Hungarian reconnaissance unit lost in the Alps. In the poem, the soldiers faced an icy death until their leader found a map which he used to lead the platoon to safety. On their return, however, it was found that the map was not of the Alps but of the Pyrenees.

"We considered ourselves
lost and waited for the end. And then one of us
found a map in his pocket. That calmed us down.
We pitched camp, lasted out the snowstorm and then
with the map
we discovered our bearings.
And here we are.
The lieutenant borrowed this remarkable map
and had a good look at it. It was not a map of the Alps
but of the Pyrenees."

The poem is an example of how a plan, or the map in this case, is not necessarily the route to success. In this case, the map provided them with hope and purpose. Teams need a vision or a desired future state as with the troops above, and it requires the right mind-set, attitude and behaviours. The map was the 'framework' to help them navigate towards their goal.

Regardless of whether you are in a large organisation, running a small business or coaching a sports team, you will want a team of winning mind-sets. A high-performing team has 'glue'. It is the substance that will bind your team together and create an environment for achieving results. You will need to focus on creating a winning culture rather than a trophy-winning mentality. Winning at sports is a bi-product of doing things right and it is the same in business. You'll need a holistic approach. It's not going to be an easy process, but if you follow these rules that I and other successful coaches have used to achieve success, you will be well on your way to creating a high-performance team.

Use a whole brain approach

It is estimated that about 65% of strategies fail. I believe one of the reasons for this is that strategies are often designed and developed by a personality and the preference of this personality influences the design of the strategy. This is the reason why there tends to be a bias towards a certain way of doing things. This can be in the form of an overfocus on results and processes or perhaps too much bias towards values and image. This type of thinking combined with a lack of strategic alignment is one of the main reasons why so many strategies fail. To ensure your strategy is successful it needs to be a holistic one that will incorporate a whole-brain approach. This means incorporating both left-brain and right-brain thinking or all four of the leadership preferences.

The two hemispheres have long been the study for neuroscientists and have generated much debate. Due to recent developments in technology we can now measure brain activity more effectively. There has been a lot of excitement in behavioural and cognitive neuroscience in recent years, and although it may appear as a new discourse in the world of personal and leadership development, there is solid research and science to back up the fact that the two hemispheres have specific functions that are hard-wired. There are certain skills that develop on either the left or right side of the brain. Having insight into this will affect how you utilise the strengths in your team.

The left side of the brain is analytical and logical, precise and time-sensitive. It is particularly good at conceiving and executing complicated plans. It is likely that anyone who has more of a preference for left-brain thinking will prefer planned strategy, a tight framework to avoid any uncertainty. The left side can also be associated with being controlling and unfeeling. The right brain is associated with being people focused and gentle, tends to be more emotional and at one with the natural world. The right side of the brain likes to dream and empathise. It enjoys creativity and novelty. This type of thinking is likely to generate a desire for an emergent and free flowing type of strategy. When there are two types of people working together it may cause conflict and frustration, but it can also create a very dynamic partnership.

Creativity requires you to embrace novelty, and the frontal lobes in the brain play a critical role in dealing with novelty. The prefrontal cortex defines us as social human beings and can have direct influence on leadership capability. Another interesting fact is that the frontal lobes continue to develop in adults through to their late twenties. This explains why decision-making improves thus improving leadership performance. It also explains why athletes come of age in their late twenties and sometimes early thirties, provided they stay fit and healthy. Ryan Giggs of Manchester United Football Club is a perfect example of this type of development. Decision-making plays a key role in sports and the ability to think clearly under pressure. This is what used to be put down to 'experience'. Whilst experience plays a role, the physical development of the brain equally plays a role.

The other thing to understand about the brain is although we have discussed left and right, the front and back of the brain is also important. The back of your brain receives input from the outside world and sorts, processes and stores all of your sensory representations. The front of the brain is devoted to the processing of output. This area helps react to the data coming in. It is where you plan, strategise and sculpt your responses to the world, and it is this area in your brain that has been adapted for use in abstract thinking and planning.

I believe it is absolutely crucial when devising a strategy that the whole brain is involved in its creation; you can do this both personally and as a team. At a personal level you can force yourself to consider what you may be lacking. I am not suggesting that you force yourself to become a left-brain or right-brain thinker, but simply consider how your preference may be causing you to neglect other options. You will also be able to utilise other team members' skill sets to compensate for what is missing in your team. It is important to know that no one hemisphere of the brain is better or more useful than the other; the fact is that they are complementary, which gives the brain its power. So my belief is that when devising a strategy the key to the success of the strategy is ensuring that all preferences are being utilised.

CHAPTER 10

FIVE RULES FOR CREATING A HIGH-PERFORMANCE TEAM

The following methodology is based on my own experiences and what I have learnt from others, both good and bad. This includes my role as Head Coach for the British Inline Hockey team, as a sales manager and my work with a number of teams I have coached in both the sports and business arena during the last ten years. A lot of thought and research has gone into the methodology to ensure that it has substance and a practical application. I have worked with teams around the world who have achieved great success creating a high performance culture and a 'mist-free' environment following these five rules, they are:

1. Get your house in order
2. Ask them, don't tell them
3. Make yourself redundant
4. Embrace failure
5. Hold them accountable

Rule #1 - Get Your House in Order

'Get your house in order' is a metaphor for creating a holistic team strategy. It ensures that your team will be dynamic by applying a 'whole brain' approach. An organisation will only be as good as the teams within it and an individual will only be as good as the team he or she is in. Therefore the quality of the team drives both the performance of the organisation and the individual. The same framework applies if you are coaching a sports team.

As you can see from the diagram there are five sections to the house. It currently looks empty; there is no vision or purpose. There aren't any clear objectives or processes. The behaviours and values are nowhere to be seen. It appears to be vacant – many teams can feel this way. Despite lots of activity there isn't any real clarity around goals, structure and mission. During this chapter I will show you how to fill the house with excitement, purpose and engagement. Whilst you'll want to create a harmonious and focused culture, great teams aren't just about camaraderie, they are also about conflict and learning how to perform under pressure. All five sections are required for creating a holistic strategy that ensures 'whole-brain thinking'. It draws on all types of behavioural preferences as described in Part Two such as results, process, values and image. You can also see that there is a left section (results and process) and a right section (values and image) to illustrate the two hemispheres of the brain.

As you begin to get your house in order and establish your team vision, the next step will be to unpick your vision and turn it into tangible results and objectives. Once you are clear on the output the next step is to create systems and processes that will ensure clarity and consistency. This could be in the form of Key Performance Indicators (KPIs). Occasionally people get objectives and KPIs confused. One way to separate the two is by using a sausage machine as analogy. (If you can think of a different analogy than a sausage machine please email me on andrew@managingthemist.com. In a results-driven environment you may focus on the quality of the sausage (result) and neglect the quality and maintenance of the machine (system). When the quality of the sausage drops, the focus shifts to trying to improve the sausage. The problem is not the sausage; the poor performance has been caused by neglecting the machine, i.e. the process. Furthermore, the neglect is often caused by poor behaviour, and as discussed in Chapter Two, behaviour drives performance! Now the goal is to fix the problem, which will eat into your precious time. A consistent performance is met when there is a focus on maintaining the system, not forcing the result.

A bias towards results and process is associated with left-brain activity. It is very common to find a left-brain thinker in a management role. Ironically, later in that person's career the company spends lots of money putting the leader through courses to help develop their emotional intelligence, i.e. right-brain thinking. Once the results have been identified the next step is to agree the type of behaviours and values of the team. This will define the culture and is essential in creating a high-performance team. The final step is to decide how you want your team to be seen, what you want people saying about you. This could be key clients, team supporters or senior management. When you have in place a vision, results, process, values and an image you will be well on your way to getting your house in order. You won't achieve success unless you apply the other four rules for creating a high-performance team.

Right-brain thinkers make good leaders but often don't make it through the management roles due to their lack of preference towards measurement and process. Left-brain thinkers have a preference towards achievement, logic, dominance, control and managing day-to-day activity, whereas right-brain thinkers tend to have a preference towards novelty, empathy, support, innovation, creativity and variety. Leaders with this preference will have a focus on driving the culture, the image of the team and their own personal branding. Left-brainers may have a more rational, planned, long-term approach, whereas the right-brainers will look for quick rewards and excitement. This may explain why the high in demand leadership trait 'charisma' is associated with the latter although obtaining it does not necessarily make for a better leader!

The fact is we need both hemispheres of the brain involved in a strategy and what you don't have yourself you can find in someone else. This is what makes certain business partnerships so effective, such as Bill Gates and Steve Ballmer of Microsoft. They complement each other; it is as if the two hemispheres form the Yin and Yang of their empire, creating a dynamic duo. Often leaders allow their ego to get in the way and they don't allow them to share ideas, best practice. They become protective in an attempt to have all the glory to themselves. They haven't realised that the potential for long-term success is more likely when collaboration takes place.

I have experienced this first-hand with a number of my clients. They will want to achieve their personal and team goals in a certain way. I have to help them become aware of their bias towards certain outcomes and help them think more holistically about their team. Another thing to mention when dealing with consultants and performance coaches is that they also have a bias and this may influence how they work with you to form a strategy.

Taking into consideration that individual motivation will vary in your team, the key to a successful team vision is to make sure that everyone has an emotional connection to the vision. They become aware of what it will mean to them personally when the vision is achieved. As with Team GB, I have run a number of workshops around the world helping teams identify with their vision.

Start with a VISION

Getting your house in order starts with a vision. A high-performance team is one that has purpose and direction. If your team is part of a larger organisation, it will need to be strategically aligned to the business goals. To achieve this you will need to identify with a desired future state and vision, you'll need to agree what 'great' is and create a desire to move away from the current position, i.e. 'good'.

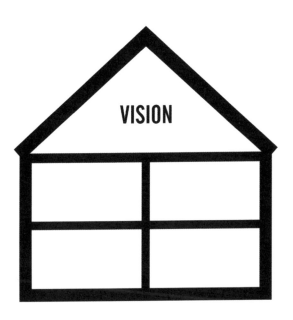

The biggest challenge for you isn't helping individuals and teams achieve their goal; it is helping them to believe a goal is possible in the first place. Developing an inspiring vision gaining 'buy-in' to the vision is crucial. Buy-in doesn't just mean agreement, it means ownership and accountability. A vision will give you and your team purpose, it will provide direction and enable you to focus on what you want to achieve, both personally and as a team.

Sports teams focus so much on winning cups, medals and titles that they forget what it takes to win in the first place! Winning doesn't just happen on the rink or pitch: it happens in every area. On Team GB, our equipment manager is as important as our top goal-scorer, and every player knows this. There is no man on the team that is indispensable. It is the same in business. Sales teams would not be able to perform as well if it weren't for the support functions, such as information technology, human resources and marketing. All parts of the system are functioning together towards a common purpose. If one part of the system changes, everything changes.

This is what I refer to as a high-performance culture: a culture and system where players are self-motivated, give as much to the team as possible, put their necks on the line for each other and will do whatever they can to improve performance. A hockey puck weighs five ounces and travels at speeds of over a hundred miles an hour. I have seen players throw their bodies in front of the puck to block shots; this type of mentality is self-directed, it is behaviour that is driven from an intrinsic desire to support one another and do whatever it takes to achieve the goal. This is the difference between winning and losing and will give any team its competitive advantage. Teams are all the same whether it is in business or an amateur sports team. What will inspire you to put your neck on the line for your teammates? Strong leadership skills are required from you to develop a high-performance culture, but it won't necessarily need your direction. Ultimately, it is your team members who need to decide on a vision and therefore leadership will be shared amongst the team.

Your team members are the ones who need to agree what they want to achieve. They will need to take into account factors such as where they are now and what needs to be done to improve their performance. Most importantly, they need to identify what it will feel like when they achieve their vision and start feeling that way today, just as the traders described in chapter 2 had to feel like traders to become successful.

I find it fascinating when a manager asks me to run a vision day for their team or business. I often hear a director say: "Andrew, we'd like you to come in and help us define our vision, perhaps you could come in for a couple of hours in the afternoon, flesh out what our vision is and then we plan to go out for a few drinks, you're more than welcome to join us." Nothing really got achieved except for a hangover. Come Monday morning it was business as usual, apart from the fact the manager had laminated the vision and put it around the office for everyone to ignore.

An effective vision requires more than just a few words and a good night out. Whether it is your personal or your team vision, it needs a strategy or framework and not just a plan or process with a number to hit. It requires a holistic strategy that incorporates a 'whole-brain approach', which we will discuss later in this chapter.

Your vision should be specific, measurable and time-bound – for example: "By January 1st 2013 we will be the highest performing team in the business." The vision will need to be unpicked into results and objectives. What is imperative at this stage is that you make a personal connection to the vision. They must identify with what it means to them in the way of rewards, which may not always be extrinsic or materialistic items, as mentioned earlier in the chapter on motivations.

Managing Change

Moving from good to great involves change, and a team going through change may experience some pain and even a dip in performance. I'd experienced change on a number of levels when working towards my own goals; it nearly caused me to give up on my goal entirely. In 1994 I was asked to play for the London Allstars, a selection of 12 players that would travel to Florida to play in a tournament. I couldn't believe it when I got the call, I thought: This is it, I've made it. All expenses paid for trip to the USA! It was incredible. I would be playing with my heroes who I had been watching on television six years prior. I remember the feeling of being in the same dressing room as the 'Axe Man', 'The General'.. It doesn't get much better than this. I had fulfilled my dream or at least that's what I thought at 17! The trip was an important moment in my life; having lost my father the previous year it gave me something to focus my attention on. It was at the point when Jock became a prominent figure in my life and helped me with my training programme. The trip gave me a purpose and I needed it at the time. The team trained every Friday in North London which meant a 130-mile round trip from Tunbridge Wells. Our coach was ruthless, we trained so hard. The coach had a huge focus on fitness and conditioning. He pushed us to breaking point and I loved every minute of it. I was used to it having trained with Jock for the previous two years. I had a learned what my body was capable of and knew that I could push it further.

We trained for three months prior to leaving for Florida. The sport was played differently in America. It was the mid 1990s and inline skates were the big fad, as was lycra, and getting fit on skates was very popular. The sport was referred to as roller hockey and heavily influenced by ice hockey. Roller hockey was becoming big business with better equipment and a professional league. At the time we were still on traditional roller skates, 'quads'. We did OK in the tournament, making the semi-finals where we lost against Palm Beach. Unfortunately, we couldn't keep up with the speed of the players, the inline skates were so much faster, more fluid and created a very different game tactically, and something we couldn't compete with.

It was a great trip and for about a year after returning I kept thinking about my experience. My goal was to play in America for a professional team; if I were to achieve that, I knew I would need to change my equipment and start using inline skates. In 1997, along with two other players, I made the switch. It was one of the most challenging and embarrassing experiences I have undertaken: we looked ridiculous, sliding everywhere, unable to stop on the thinner wheels. The rest of the hockey community thought it was a joke, questioning why some of the top players in the country would do this. In Europe we were up and coming and then overnight we were nowhere near the mark. The European teams took great pleasure in seeing us fail.

I found it very challenging and there was a time when my ego was getting the better of me. I questioned if we were doing the right thing, we had a few casualties that weren't prepared to make the change and stopped playing entirely. I considered going back to my quad skates where I was in my comfort zone, but as I mentioned earlier I was fortunate to play on the team with a group of people who exemplified a winning mind-set. I was part of a group of people who had a vision to be the number one team in Europe. A single organising thought that created a relentless desire to succeed. We were a good team and we wanted to be a great team.

Despite being amateur and all having our day jobs, we had team training three nights a week. On a Sunday night we travelled for 90 minutes just so we could practise at a facility that would give us a competitive advantage. It was never a chore, players pushed each other, we fell out with each other, we made up and we became stronger. Conflict is part of the process to becoming a high-performance team and we had a fair share of arguments.

After battling with the change of equipment, the arguments, the dip in performance, the Tunbridge Wells Street Cruisers dominated for three years in both the UK and in Europe. We won three major international tournaments, beating the Dusseldorf Rams who had dominated the sport for so many years. Like the London Allstars experience in 1994 against Palm Beach, we were now too fast, too fluid and tactically a very different team. We continued to dominate the sport domestically and in Europe whilst other teams played catch-up, making the same transition to inline skates. Despite the remarks, and the mocking for wearing inline skates, it is now extremely rare to see a single player on traditional quad skates!

Moving from good to great will be challenging for you, change is painful but there is reward. You will have to embrace change and the pain that comes with it to achieve your goal. Nothing can prepare you for the pain, but the pain itself will prepare you for the future. In return it makes the success even more rewarding. Sometimes when I look back at the pain it was the best part!

Get the RESULTS

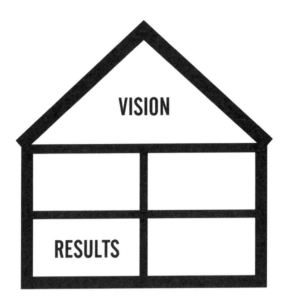

Let's start with results – is your organisation a results-driven company? That may sound obvious, most companies are these days. Most companies are looking at ways to drive the bottom line and increase profit. When was the last time your boss asked you how much you have developed in your role? It's more likely that they asked you how the figures are looking. How is their personality driving the behaviour of the company? How much is their preference having an influence on the strategic direction? This may be a sweeping statement, but most people who get into senior positions have done so because they are competitive, focused on delivery and want to 'win' the next promotion. Not always the best leader, by the way.

In actual fact, the best leaders I have met, albeit results-driven, take less notice of the results and pay more attention to processes and the behaviours required for success. They allow the results to speak for themselves. You will need to agree the goals as a team and what you are aiming for. These results and objectives will be milestones and provide you with the ability to measure progress, celebrate wins and maintain confidence that you are on the right track. Talk about the reality of where the team's current performance is and discuss the opportunities for improvement. Ask what needs to change. You may find that you don't have the talent – maybe you'll need to recruit. Don't limit yourself to what you can achieve with what you have; aim high and find, develop and keep what you need to achieve your vision.

When unpicking your vision into results you may find that you come up with lots of results that you want to achieve. When doing this for yourself or with your team, you can generate as many as you like, the key is to identify with four or five that will really have an impact. The results will need to be specific, measurable and within a certain timeframe and they must contribute to the organisational goals. This is especially key when you want to align your team or business to your strategy as you'll want everyone in your organisation aligned, working towards a common goal. Strategic alignment is not easy, it takes a lot of work and it is crucial for driving successful strategy. If you cannot implement it don't do it. Broadcasting from the top won't cut it!

Know the PROCESS

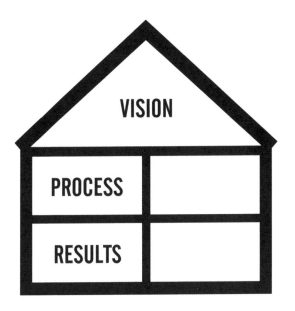

You now have a vision which has been broken down into results; the next step is to create a process or system (a machine) that will deliver the results. Hang in there if you're a right-brain thinker, this is not the time to stop reading this book; process may seem dull for you but a good process is key for achieving consistency. With a fully committed team on board, your next step to any successful strategy is to establish how you will do it. It is at this point when you can bring your experience to the table, implementing a specific framework or process. Although direction from you is needed to put this process in place successfully, I would recommend having involvement to create awareness on their behalf. Ask them questions such as:

"What processes need to be in place to achieve our goals?"
"What will the key performance indicators be?"
"How will we measure the quality of what we are doing?"

Don't let your ego get in the way. You may know the answers, be patient. You will be surprised at how insightful your team members are, even those new to your team or the business. You will gain more credibility and support when you include them in the decision-making process. Many organisations I have worked in are obsessed with process and planning to the point where it stifles creativity. As with strategy, I prefer to call processes frameworks, this way you can create autonomy and freedom to work within the framework, i.e. 'freedom in the framework'. Frameworks create certainty and this is important to some people. If your CEO is particularly driven by certainty, perhaps risk averse, he or she will like to use KPIs and a systematic approach to performance. Whilst it is important, it can sometimes appear stifling and reduce creativity and autonomy. You may also find that you have hit KPIs just for KPIs' sake, which really is an attempt to control performance not develop it.

The key to implementing successful processes and performance indicators is to align them to the results, which are of course aligned to the vision. This way, when you are setting individual objectives it is clear that they are aligned to the bigger picture. People no longer wonder why they are doing what they are doing, they have line of sight all the way up the company and feel like they are helping the organisation achieve its corporate strategy. My belief is this is why many strategies fail, because they fail to align their people with a common goal. This may sound obvious but it is the reason, according to one study, why 90% of strategies that are developed don't get implemented.

In sports a lot of inexperienced players find it hard to play systems; it takes patience, confidence and clear thinking. Players that have results preference tend to get impatient and want to move in the most direct route, which is usually to the opponent's net to create a scoring opportunity. I see this in business too, especially in sales where sales people lack lateral thinking and become so focused on achieving the result they lose sight of the quality of the process, which is affected by poor behaviour. When they don't get what they want they become frustrated and angry and do more of the same, or start riding the 'emotional roller coaster'. Therefore driving the right behaviour is essential for delivering a quality performance.

A process or system will create certainty, understanding and awareness amongst your team. Encourage your team members to focus on the system and allow the results to happen. To ensure they are aligned you simply work with each result that needs to be achieved and create a process that will deliver those results. Processes, systems, frameworks – whatever you want to call them – are commonly used in team sports. They create awareness and clarity amongst team members. I am a great believer in using systems or frameworks in sport as long as they allow for freedom and autonomy to enable creativity within the framework. The same must be said in business too.

When I coached Team GB in 2011 we had five main areas that needed to be addressed in the way of results. There are a number of other performance indicators involved but these are frameworks I am using to illustrate my point: 1. Move the puck out of our end fast; 2. Maintain possession of the puck in our opponent's end; 3. Clog the 'neutral zone' (midfield area); 4. Contain and trap opposition in our opponent's end; 5. Contain and dispossess the puck in our end (zone defence) – all with the aim of creating a scoring opportunity, thus making us offensive whilst being defensively orientated. I created five systems to meet the needs of the required results. I also created an extra system for each area to mitigate any risk of the system collapsing through the opposition attempting to break it down. As coach, all I needed to see from where I was standing was that the players were implementing the system. This indicated that we were thinking and doing the right things on the rink. I knew the results would speak for themselves. You will want to able to observe from the bench too, you'll want comfort that your team is doing all the right things. To use the house analogy, you will knock on the door occasionally and see how things are going, and most important of all you'll want to be sure that they are demonstrating the right behaviours.

Drive the BEHAVIOUR

I know that I have said it several times already: behaviour drives performance! It doesn't matter how much skill you have in your team, or even experience, if the appropriate behaviours are not in place it will all be wasted. Now that you have a vision, results to achieve the vision and solid processes to deliver the results, without the right behaviours your team will not achieve its full potential. You may find with results and systems that it works for a period of time but eventually your team will fall apart without the correct behaviours driving them. The left brain simply isn't enough!

Behaviour and attitude can account for as much as 80% of performance, leaving 20% between skills and knowledge. I find it amazing that managers and coaches focus 80% of their time developing skills when it only accounts for 10-20% of the performance. If you want a high-performing team, focus your attention on the 80% that will really make a difference: behaviour!

The biggest driver for me when it comes to achieving results is behaviour. As a coach, a lot of time and energy can be wasted trying to 'motivate' a team of individuals. You will need to inspire the players to exceed their own expectations. As with professional sport, business performance is 80% mind-set.

Behaviour is a manifestation of the personalities within your team. Your team will have a personality. The aim is to gain buy-in from all the personalities and align their behaviour to the team vision. Also remember that the individual team members have made a personal connection to the vision. You will have also asked them what life will be like if nothing changes and therefore creating urgency to move away from the current state. Asking what behaviours are conducive to creating a high-performance team at this stage should be straightforward. The majority of human beings know what is right and what is wrong; they are able to make effective decisions about behaviour. If they can't, then they probably shouldn't be on your team! Amazingly, studies into neuroscience have shown that a baby can innately tell the difference between good and bad by the age of six months, so an adult has no excuse for poor behaviour! When I recruit, my final decision will be based on their behaviour not how good they are technically.

Driving organisational and team behaviour must be more than a human resources initiative. Creating the right behaviour isn't just about doing things right, it is about creating an environment where people have freedom to get things wrong and learn. Whilst performance goals are important, setting behavioural and development goals is even more important. When you coach your people, consider what development goals are required rather than discussing results or KPIs. For example, rather than asking a sales person to make 20 calls in the next two hours, ask them to improve their use of open questions for the next two hours. It will distract them from the pressure and boredom of making the calls and encourage them to focus on quality and performance improvement. If you ask any player on Team GB how many times I worked on their skills, they are likely to say never. Through driving behaviours you will drive sustainable results. It is fair to say that I have the luxury of picking the best players in the country, and to a certain extent so do you. How you select your talent is an essential part of your team strategy but, regardless of this, whoever is on your team will need to exhibit the right behaviours and values to be a high-performance team. You will achieve more sustainable results with a group of people who exhibit behavioural excellence and meet the skill threshold than you will out of a highly skilled team who don't meet the behavioural threshold.

Once you have managed to get your team to identify with the right behaviours required to deliver results that will help achieve your vision, and you have engaged them in the whole decision-making process, you are well on your way to creating a high-performance team. Be sure to allow them the freedom to make mistakes, be there when they need your support and coach them. Encourage them to embrace failure rather than avoid it.

It's all about IMAGE

Whenever I am coaching a team, an individual or even an organisation I always ask them to think of two people they admire, and if I hear them having a conversation in the corridor and they are talking about those people, I ask: "What would you like to hear them say about you or your team?" The aim here is to start thinking about your external image.

Image and branding is more important to some than others. Image may not be important to you but image and branding at both personal and team level is a key factor when developing a holistic strategy. The aim is to define what you stand for – what do you want people saying about you? How do you want to be seen by others? What is your mission statement? This is to help you hone in on what it will take to achieve your vision and goals. It moves the strategy to an external focus and perception whereas most of what we have talked about is internally focused.

Left-brain thinkers or introverts may not pay as much attention to this area. Introverts tend to have less of a concern for what people think about them. It is very important to consider external perception. You don't have to be an extrovert to have a focus on external branding, especially at an individual level. When you are planning your career, how you network and appear to others will be integral to your success whether you like it or not; as mentioned earlier, this is essential when developing your presence. Once you have identified with what those two people will be saying about you when you achieve your vision, write it down and pick out key words, you can then start to form a mission statement. The statement may be in the form of one to two sentences. Some of my clients have come up with a way that describes them in just one word.

Often companies confuse vision with mission statements. A vision is a future desired state, whereas a mission is how you will achieve it. It may not accurately describe your current performance but it will become self-fulfilling if you start acting that way today. For example, a professional athlete doesn't wait until they are professional before they start acting as a professional. They act professionally when they are amateur and then gaining professional status is the result. Your branding is important but there is a caveat: you will need to back it up with consistent results. I see a lot of organisations that are good at creating a great image but lack the drive, process and behaviours to support that image.

VALUES

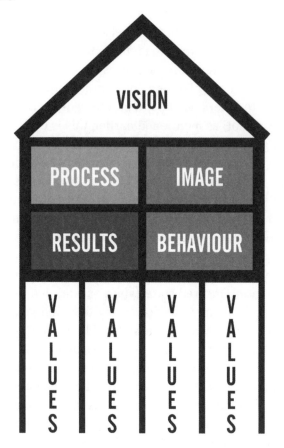

Your house is nearly in order but without values it is built on sloppy sand. Team values are the foundations for driving the right behaviours. Getting the right core set of values is the key to success: values are integral in creating an environment for winning. Your team members will need to believe in the values and the values will need to be aligned to their own personal values rather than being just a set of words. They have to live and breathe them.

The big success story for Team GB Inline Hockey in 2011 was adopting the values of its sponsor – energy, respect, rapport and reward – which we wore proudly on our team shirts and clothing. These words were fundamental in shaping the culture of the team. I was surprised at how well the team embraced the values into everything we did on and off the rink. We ran a number of workshops to help the players connect personally with the values so that they became more than just words on a poster or a team shirt. Interestingly, when I was at a sports awards night in London at the end of 2011, I was seated at a table next to an HR specialist from the Football Association. I was sharing my experience with Team GB and the community work we had done applying the team values. She was commenting on how she thought the FA should look into creating some values. It's interesting – I don't see values anywhere on the England shirts or in the way of some of their behaviours. You make of that what you will.

There are a number of ways to instil values into your team. Ultimately it will have to be role modelled by you. You will have to exemplify the behaviours you expect to see in your team. If you want your team to be composed, you will have to be. If you want your team to treat each other with respect, you will have to be respectful at all times. You can undo a lot of hard work by not displaying the right behaviours. You'll need to exemplify the behaviours you want to see in your team. If you don't you will lose credibility and you are unlikely to get the best out of your people.

Now that you have your house in order and created a holistic strategy, the following four rules will help shape the strategy fully, ensuring that you have engaged every team member and have their full commitment.

Rule 2 - Ask them, don't tell them

*"People have innate knowledge, they just need
to be asked the right question."*
Plato

The concept of asking, rather than telling, is nothing new. It was Steven Covey, author of *The 7 Habits of Highly Successful People* who said: *"First seek to understand before being understood"* (1998). Unfortunately, this skill is not used enough. It is a basic coaching skill, but typically in a fast-moving environment spending time coaching is one of the first things to disappear from a leader's toolbox. Instead, leaders move towards a directive style of communication and this approach is a short-term gain for a long-term loss. The biggest barrier to coaching is time. Managers regularly tell me that they can't afford the time with their people; my response is always the same: "You can't afford not to spend time with your people." Coaching doesn't have to be an hour-long conversation; with the right technique and skills you will be amazed at what you can achieve in ten minutes. I run a short coaching clinic named 'The Power of Ten Minutes' helping managers and leaders frame a pragmatic, goal orientated conversation that when managed properly and done regularly (a minimum of once a week) will dramatically increase the performance of an individual. You will be amazed at what you will learn about your people and how motivated they will become off the back of a focused conversation.

Be a High-Performance Coach

Although my coaching experience stems back to 1992 when coaching sports teams, I didn't start personal and business coaching until 2004. I have found that most of my life lessons have been through learning more about other people and being curious about what they want out of life. Since qualifying as a coach I have become more self-aware, enhanced my leadership skills, improved team results and created winning mind-sets through what I have learned from coaching others. Coaching has become a well-established industry, widely accepted today and one of the fastest growing industries in the world. Type 'coaching' into a search engine and you will find a plethora of coaches to choose from, such as life coaches, performance coaches, executive coaches, neurocoaches the list goes on. Coaching and mentoring are important skills to learn if you are looking to drive results through people.

If you work for an organisation it is likely that they are soliciting external coaches to support the executives and managers in your business. Furthermore, you and your peers are also expected to develop your own coaching prowess in order to develop your teams, which I firmly encourage. Coaching or mentoring is a way to help someone find his or her own solutions, and at a team level you are more likely to create engagement into the vision. The key to being a good coach is listening, rapport-building and questioning. Questioning is at the core of good coaching. Californian-based tennis coach and coaching guru Timothy Gallwey defines coaching as:

"Coaching is unlocking a person's potential to maximise their own performance. It is helping them to learn rather than teaching them."

In his book *The Inner Game of Tennis* (1973), Gallwey challenged the prevalent method of sports coaching in the early 1970s where tennis coaches were 'telling' players how to play the game and filling their heads with complex information, which he referred to as 'interference'. His formula of Performance = Potential - Interference (P=P-I) proposes that humans have unlimited potential and the role of a coach is to remove interference or internal dialogue that may prevent someone from performing at their best. By interference, Gallwey was referring to the 'inner critic'. You have one, I have one, and everybody has one. The role of the coach is to help remove the negativity coming from the inner voice and replace it with something conducive for reaching their full potential.

Gallwey's approach was initially received as 'Californian mumbo jumbo'. However, he proved its worth by demonstrating the theory on a live TV show in the US with huge success. The idea of facilitating learning rather than telling seems a mature approach to developing people and a departure from didactic methods often seen in businesses and in sports. The following quotes sum up coaching nicely and suggests this approach is nothing new and dates back to ancient Greek philosophy over 2,000 years ago:

> *"You cannot teach a man anything; you can only help him to find it within himself."*
> Galileo

> *"People have innate knowledge, they just need to be asked the right question."*
> Plato

When I accepted the role as head coach for Team Great Britain, they had previously struggled to compete with teams such as Austria and Slovenia having never beaten them in the past. I made the fatal mistake of going in all guns blazing and meeting a new generation of hockey players head on. I stated very early on that no man was indispensable, and just because they made the team last year it didn't mean they would make the team this year. Whilst this was true, I really should have settled in a little first. I should have taken the time to find out more and learn about the players, understand their experiences and motivations. I certainly didn't embrace Covey's habit: 'Seek first...'

Players had heard about my philosophy on how I would select the team based on behaviour over skills. They felt threatened and practically boycotted playing for me at first. Several key players didn't show up for the first training session. I remember that I had just read Clive Woodward's book titled *Winning*. In it he shares how he bought laptops for the England team players so they could communicate with each other. I decided I would get some communication going amongst the players, so I sent out a number of group emails and wasn't getting any responses. Unknown to me at the time, this was partly due to the fact that the team comprised mostly Generation Y, often referred to as Gen Y (born between 1980-2000).

They didn't use email, this was considered 'old school'. They used Facebook instead to communicate. So we started to communicate via a group on Facebook which has worked very well. Players could upload videos of their training regimes, updates on their progress and share best practice. It also created some rivalry and healthy competition in the team.

Gen Y is perceived to have a disregard for authority and being selfish. This was certainly my initial point of view based on my interaction with Team GB; since then I have learned how to get the best out of Gen Y. You may need to challenge your assumptions about Gen Y and ask yourself what you can change about yourself rather than how to change Gen Y. Societies change and we have to learn to change with them. Trying to force a new generation to think your way, which is ultimately influenced by the environment you were raised in, will only be met with frustration on both sides. Initially I was frustrated and my frustration was further increased when one of the players sent me a list of the players that he thought should be on the team, including himself of course! This is quite typical of Gen Y. Don't be surprised if a fresh grad in your business tries to arrange a meeting with your CEO to discuss the future of the business. Generation Y have ideas and they want to be heard.

What I was doing wasn't working. I had acquired an underperforming team. GB had lost to Australia in the quarter-finals the previous year and morale was low. I made promises that we would win gold and gain promotion into the A Pool, a feat that Team GB had never achieved before. Team GB had never beaten Austria, which was our biggest barrier, but I knew it was a mind-set issue not a skill issue. The first mind-set change was going to be my own. It was a different generation that I was engaging with and it required a different approach from me. I asked myself a question I had read somewhere years before: Are you looking outside the window asking the questions or are you looking in the mirror and asking the questions? It was clear to me that the responsibility for change lay with me. I immediately changed my strategy: I started asking them rather than telling them. I started to take on the role of coach not dictator; I acted more as a facilitator rather than forcing my own agenda and vision onto them.

I ran several workshops to get all the players together to flesh out the vision before moving on to forming the strategy on how to win Pool B. Here are examples of the questions I used. It's important to keep it simple at the initial stage.

- What is our goal?

- What do you want to achieve on this team?

- What will that look, feel and sound like to you when it is achieved?

- What will it look, feel and sound like on Team GB if nothing changes? (Create a desire for change)

- What needs to change/take place in order to achieve the goals?

We created a team vision and rather than setting our sights on winning Pool B, we focused our strategy on a vision for us to aim for, 'Look, act and feel like a Pool A team'. By doing this we aimed to raise the level beyond winning Pool B. During the workshop the players became highly engaged, far more than I anticipated. They wrote their personal goals on flip charts and how they wanted to be communicated to by the coaching staff and players. They identified the type of conditioning and training they would need to implement in order to reach their personal goals. The squad members presented back to the rest of the players and staff. The players were applauding each other and respect for each other was growing by the minute.

They were at the beginning of creating and owning the strategy for Team GB and they were moving from 'good' to 'great'. As head coach I was merely facilitating the interaction. I also used phrases like: "I have absolutely no doubt that you will achieve this" and "This team has unlimited potential, don't let your way of thinking hold you back." Even if I had a little doubt myself, who am I to doubt anyone else? As I mentioned earlier, the biggest challenge isn't achieving the goal, it is helping your team believe it is possible in the first place. When your team creates a vision, don't stop at what they think is possible. If there is one main role of a leader, it is to inspire others to go beyond their own expectations. So when you set your personal or team vision, set it high, be a little deluded – you may surprise yourself at what you can achieve. In the words of Michelangelo:

"The greater danger for most of us lies not in setting our aim too high and falling short but in setting our aim too low, and achieving our mark."

Rule 3 - Make Yourself Redundant

This concept is based on the idea that leadership is shared amongst a team and every member plays a role in the decision-making. It assumes that when the parts form a whole it creates behaviour of its own. It is as if the team has a brain of its own. The team is developing, thinking and behaving like a single entity. The more joined-up thinking and single organising thought your team has, the more effective it will be. To implement shared leadership successfully will require huge amounts of trust from you, as well as patience and strong facilitation skills. Facilitation skills are an underestimated leadership skill and should be developed along with performance coaching skills. These skills will enhance your leadership and the development of your team.

The best performing teams I have seen are when every member has contributed towards the team strategy. Different individuals who held different individual strengths took turns in running training sessions or team meetings. They had a shared vision and over time developed an intuitive approach to decision-making; all decisions were made in the best interest of reaching their goals and implementation of their strategy. This is an example of successful 'shared leadership'. Shared leadership challenges whether leadership is even necessary at all or at least perception of leadership may need reviewing.

In the past I managed a team of leadership consultants for a large organisation across the UK and mainland Europe. The team had experienced a number of changes in the business. I was fortunate that I had an experienced group of consultants. I applied a shared style of leadership. However, my leadership style has been described as non-directive and I had some feedback that there was a need for more directive leadership from me. Does this suggest that shared leadership may not be the appropriate style during turbulent and uncertain times? On the contrary, if shared leadership is being implemented effectively, it is during uncertain times that decision-making amongst team members is crucial.

On reflection, it is fair to say that we didn't have our house in order, for which I take responsibility. We didn't identify clearly what our vision and the strategy were. In sports it is easy: win gold or the championships etc. It is more difficult in business but you can achieve it as long as you have a vision. Someone will step up to the plate and take ownership. When a team is under pressure it relies on someone to raise their game. The responsibility doesn't always have to rest on the shoulders of the manager. Someone will surprise you. In fact I think we should drop the word manager entirely! Even if you're not in a leadership role, it doesn't stop you developing leadership behaviours today. I wish someone had told me this earlier in my career.

A team that I worked with in the Netherlands sales division of a large recruitment business described their managing director as being ahead of his time. This was due to his focus on people and how he has increased the autonomy and shared leadership amongst his team, which was atypical of the direct, results-driven approach to management prevalent across the organisation. He is now a global leader for an international recruitment company. The idea of applying shared leadership is relatively new in comparison to traditional management thinking, which has its roots stemming from the Industrial Revolution. During the last 100 years we have witnessed many types of management theory, such as Taylor's Scientific Management, Blanchard's Situational Leadership to Goleman's theory on Emotional Intelligence. There have been over 10,000 books written on the subject. This book was never intended to be an addition to the array of available leadership books – however, it is a book on enhancing personal and team performance.

It may seem angelic to think of a leader exhibiting selfless acts and not taking any credit for the glory. My view is if your team thinks they have achieved success and believe they were entirely responsible, you have demonstrated great leadership. Although the idea of creating a shared vision and sharing responsibility is good leadership and should be encouraged, there is a caveat here. For shared leadership to be successful it will require a strong, trusted and talented team, it will require that you recruit the right talent in the right positions, so how you recruit and develop talent in your team will need to be thought through carefully. You may have to be ruthless with your decision-making. Some people simply aren't right for the job or position and in some cases you may be doing them a favour by letting them go.

Rule 4 - Embrace Failure

Earlier we discussed the concept of embracing failure to help improve personal performance. As a leader you will also need to create a 'mist-free' environment for your people to thrive. The aim is create a relaxed and focused mentality. When was the last time your boss asked you how many mistakes you have made? Has anyone ever set mistakes as a KPI? Unlikely. I always ask how many mistakes someone has made. Mistakes happen, it proves to me that people are stretching themselves and getting outside their comfort zone. When people make mistakes they learn; if they learn they get better and if they get better the performance of the team will improve. I'm not suggesting that you let everyone lower your standards. What I am encouraging is an environment where people feel relaxed and accepting failure is a possibility. A relaxed and focused team will perform better than a stressed and distracted team. When I first started to work with the GB team I noticed how a number of players didn't seem relaxed on the puck. These were elite players who you'd expect to be performing at their best. There was a particular system that I wanted them to execute effectively, but they just weren't implementing it. I knew that it would be the difference between winning and losing for us, especially against teams like Hungary and Austria.

One of our mantras was 'playing safe is risky' and they were playing safe. Now there are times when it is appropriate to play safe but is also a sign of withdrawal from a perceived threat and that is not good; when a team starts to withdraw it is a sign of fear and the opposition can smell it. At the end of practice I asked them what the problem was with executing the play, which basically involved 'cycling' the puck in our opponent's end to maintain possession of the puck. The thing is they have to be aggressive and set picks on the opponent and it can leave us vulnerable defensively. When I asked them why they were being timid and playing safe, they responded by saying they were concerned that if we lost possession in their end they would counter-attack us. I asked them what the worst case scenario was. "They will score!" they replied. "Yes that is correct," I responded. I continued: "We are going to get scored on in games. Teams are not going to roll over and give us a win. And yes we need to mitigate our risk." I knew that if they made the play properly we would be defensively sound. The problem was their 'inner critic' was telling them that something might go wrong. The aim is to respond to the inner critic and say "Yes you are right and I'm OK with that." Once they had identified with the problem and put it into perspective, they became more relaxed and focused on what needed to be done rather than what might go wrong. They went back on to the rink and they looked like a different team. When you are in the 'zone' time seems slower, you have clarity and things just seem to bounce your way. As a coach or leader you don't want your team to be tense and stressed – this will cause anxiety and poor performance. As we know, the constant rush of cortisol and adrenaline in the body is not healthy. It may protect you in the short term but it is not sustainable; you and your team will find yourselves riding the emotional roller coaster when you really want to be delivering consistent results.

Mistakes are OK

I noticed how tense the Team GB players were in the dressing room before they played their first game of the World Championships in 2011 against Australia. Australia knocked out Team GB in the quarter-finals the previous year and no matter what sport, GB never likes to lose to our commonwealth rivals down under. During lunch the captain asked me how I thought the game would go, I told him that we would win 5-0 against Australia, he didn't seem too convinced. With the tension and nerves in the dressing room before the game it was unlikely that the team would perform at their full potential. I was convinced that we would beat Australia but the team would need to be relaxed to take advantage of all the hard work we had put in during the previous nine months leading up to the tournament. So in my pre-game talk I told them that with all the hard work they had put in I would allow them to make mistakes for 50% of the game, and if we made mistakes for 50% of the time we would win. In my mind I knew they would probably make mistakes for 10% of the time. It was amazing how the stress in the room disappeared and the team became more relaxed. We didn't beat Australia 5-0, we beat them 6-1; we met Australia again in the semi-final and beat them 11-3. We went on to dominate Pool B. Team GB beat Austria 7-3 – a great score considering GB had never beaten Austria in its history. GB went on to beat Hungary in the final to gain promotion into Elite 8 for the first time.

We achieved our vision – Team GB looked, acted and felt like a Pool A team. The team was able to play in a relaxed state, accepting that mistakes happen, and took action towards achieving its goals. Failure is where you learn the most and therefore you should embrace it, in fact celebrate it, because each time you experience failure and pain your performance will improve. On my debut for Team GB as a player in 1998 we lost every game. We lost to Argentina in the play-off game for relegation and didn't get to compete again for three years in the IIHF World Championships – not a bad start to my international campaign! In 2011 Team GB beat Argentina 11-0. In 2012 Team GB did the unimaginable by taking the current World Champions, the Czech Republic, into overtime. To put this into perspective, Ales Hemsky plays for the Czech Inline Team, he also plays for the National Ice Hockey Team and is a key player for the Edmonton Oilers in the NHL. He earns six million plus US dollars a year. Team GB had Kris Hendy who is a taxi driver in Brighton! Was it luck taking the Czechs into overtime? You could easily think so until Team GB beat five times world champs Finland and advanced to take on Canada in the quarter-finals.

Don't get caught up in mind games

Before the game against Canada there was so much pressure on both teams, particularly on Team Canada. The idea of losing to Team GB was unthinkable. In the round robin we had tied with the Czech team and beaten Finland. We had proved that we could compete at that level. I was absolutely convinced that we could beat Canada; I knew we had the ability and talent to steal a win. To think that Team GB lost to Argentina in 1998 is hard to believe.

The hours leading up to the game were an emotional roller coaster. Canada had made a noise about our James Tanner's pads, suggesting that he had made alterations to them, which is illegal. He hadn't at all – he had worked with the manufacturer to develop the pads so they performed better in inline; pads tend to stick in inline when goalies slide across the net to make a save, unlike on the ice. Tanner is an exceptional athlete and a massive asset to the team having just come off the back of the game against Finland taking 50 shots and conceding one, a 98% save average. Not many goalies can say that after a game against a team like Finland. On reflection, I let it get to me too much. I am the master of mind games and on this occasion I lost the game.

It was my first quarter-final in Pool A and it was a completely new experience for me. We could have found ourselves playing in the semi-final against Slovenia who had upset Sweden in the other quarter-final. We knew that we were more than capable of beating Slovenia. In fact, part of our contingency plan was to meet Slovenia in the relegation game to stay in Pool A. Another example of how planned strategy does not work! The odds of Sweden beating Slovenia are probably 20-1 in Sweden's favour. The fact was we had a chance of making the final if we could get past Canada. Team GB making the final in Pool A would have been a miracle and it was mouth-wateringly close.

It is the fateful error in sport and business to get carried away with this type of forward thinking. Whilst scenario planning is a good skill, there is a danger of not being in the here and now and truly present. Yes, it is important to have a vision, a goal and plan, albeit a flexible plan. But as soon as you lose sight of what is important in the here and now, you will become distracted – as I did and did not take the actions required to achieve success for the immediate goal, which was for us to beat Canada. The anxiety clouded my judgement. I made changes to the game plan which I thought would help us be more effective but on reflection they were unnecessary. The game did not start well; they got an early goal which created belief that Tanner was actually beatable. For us to be successful in Pool A we needed to contain teams for at least two periods, and before we could actually take a breath Canada were three goals up.

The final result was 9-3.

It was a tough loss against Canada and it raised another issue for me when the Team Canada coach and I spoke about the game the next day. As much as he is a coach, he is also deeply analytical, something that I am not. As discussed, analytical skills are associated with the left side of the brain and my preference is very much on the right side of the brain. My style of coaching is based on a strategy for creating a high-performance culture and what I see in the moment, and then applying my intuition. He showed me on video how he exploited our weaknesses. He had over four hours of video footage of our games. He talked me through in detail how he unpicked our systems and took advantage of us. It was a real eye-opener for me and despite my focus on implementing systems, this type of analysis was a whole new level. It was Pool A level, and something I have since integrated into my coaching and is a key part of our strategy. It is a good example of how a bias towards doing things a certain way can become detrimental and creates an opportunity to be even better.

Team Canada eventually went on to beat Germany in front of 7,000 screaming German fans to become the 2012 World Champions and deservedly so. We watched from the stands, relaxing with a few cold beers, safe in the knowledge we had achieved more than we ever thought possible. Team GB proved that if we aim high, are a little deluded, we can all exceed our own expectations. I observed the final, reflecting on how far Team

GB had come since our debut at the World Championships in 1998. It was also emotional to see my good friend Kirk French who I played with on the Vipers team back in 1997 become a World Champion 14 years later. For me, he epitomised what a winning mind-set is with his determination and passion for the sport. He was 35 years old and had persevered for that moment his entire hockey career.

Rule 5 - Hold Them Accountable!

"Unless commitment is made, there are only promises and hopes; but no plans."
Peter F. Drucker

The last but certainly not the least rule is holding your people accountable for the actions they have committed to. Your team has its house in order having identified with the vision, results, process, values and its image for success. You have successfully facilitated involvement from all team members by asking them what they believe is required rather than telling them. They feel engaged and motivated with a common purpose and utilising their individual strengths. They are committed and are appreciating the autonomy that you have given them. They feel relaxed without any fear of making mistakes or getting things wrong. They are so relaxed that their performance has rocketed. You have practically made yourself redundant. All you need to do now is swing by the house for coffee and make sure they achieved what they committed to when you agreed the actions with them. Your role is to hold them accountable, maintain strong relationships, measuring performance against their promises. They feel that they are doing it all by themselves, you appear invisible to them except when they need you. Your ego is absolutely fine with it and you are proud of the great work they doing, you can appreciate the intrinsic reward for cultivating a high-performance culture.

Below, the Assistant Captain Kris Hendy reflects on when Team GB won the Gold medal in 2011 and gained promotion into the A Pool of the 2012 World Championships:

"The mix of leadership and maturity was evident from the beginning. The ethos of the team was a basic fundamental from the word go. Our coaches made it clear that it was the right mind-set along with the particular skill sets that would be considered for team selection, with everything relating back to our key values, never much relating to particular individual skills. Respect was given at all times across the team, through opinions and behaviour. Certain key role models were evident – Kurt led by the way he skated and played the game, Walsh and Tanner were strong voices in the changing room and 'glue-like' personalities allowed the team to interact and bond well. Every player knew their individual roles and responsibilities and only had to look at the guy next to him to realise that they all had the same objective.

"As leaders – confidence was given from the start and remained positive throughout, with lots of positive comments, constantly reminding us that we are working towards an end goal – the Gold medal game. We were always looking to build on our mistakes or problem areas and learn from them. Our team culture/behaviour was a primary focus, eating and moving around as a team. Actions were discussed as a team and as too were player's individual movements. Attention was made as to how far we had come as a team, in constant reference, our past results do not define us, but our future conduct and play does. "We are only as good as our last game... in fact we are only as good as our next game."

As a team I felt that the team was gaining momentum from day one – player and line-ups were learning and adapting/adjusting from their mistakes without much needing to be said. Personal responsibility was being taken. Belief in our systems and chosen style of play grew as we moved forward, culminating in the semi and final games. As a player it felt like riding a wave and that the wave kept getting stronger by the day. I knew that even if one of our lines weren't firing then the other two would be! The belief that was always there was that if we stayed to our planned style of hockey, the goals would come; it was inevitability, a feeling that I have only experienced very briefly, fleetingly in games but never across a whole tournament. In the final, at the end when the buzzer went, it wasn't so much a feeling of relief of winning as in past experiences but a feeling of fulfilling our expectations. By the end of the week with this team, my thoughts going into the final were that we were no longer a pool B team and that we expected a winning result against a team which only a few years ago had looked beyond us. I knew that if we continued to play our systems and believe in our hockey then the result was inevitable."

Take action

Any group of people can exceed their own expectations. When a common goal is in place, with the right set of behaviours and shared leadership has been applied, you will see passionate group individuals working harder, going further and being truly remarkable. Going from good to great isn't easy, it can be painful but when you all look back you will be proud of what you have achieved. You'll need to get your house in order first, think holistically, create a vision, break the vision into specific, measurable and time-bound results, and put processes and systems in place to ensure quality and consistency. Agree the behaviours required for success and decide how you want to be seen by the outside world. Create a culture that embraces failure and the unknown. Let go of the ego and make yourself redundant. You will enhance your leadership ability, develop winning mind-sets and create a high-performance culture, achieving the respect that you deserve.

About the Author

Andrew is the owner of Winning Mindset Consulting Ltd, a company that is passionate about enhancing leadership, creating high-performance teams and developing winning mind-sets.

Andrew is an experienced executive coach and business consultant. He studied an MSc in 'Management Consulting and Organisational Change' at Birkbeck University and draws upon his strong commercial experience to help organisations, teams and individuals realise their potential and deliver better results.

A talented athlete, Andrew played 77 games in 11 World Championships for Great Britain Inline Hockey Team and competed professionally representing Vancouver, California and Colorado. In 2011 Andrew coached Great Britain to win a Division One gold medal, achieving promotion into the top eight countries at the IIHF 2012 World Championships for the first time.

Andrew lives in Kent with his wife Lucie and daughter Izzie, when he's not busy travelling the world helping clients 'Manage the Mist'.

andrew@managingthemist.com